THE CORPORATE MYSTIC 2.0

THE CORPORATE MYSTIC 2.0

A Guidebook for Visionaries with Their Feet on the Ground

GAY HENDRICKS, PH.D.
KATE LUDEMAN, PH.D.

Hendricks Institute Publishing

THE CORPORATE MYSTIC 2.0
The Hendricks Institute, Inc.
www.hendricks.com

All rights reserved.
Copyright © 2019 by Gay Hendricks, Ph.D.

Cover design by Patrick Broom

No part of this book may be reproduced or transmitted in any form or by any means, electronic or mechanical, including photocopying, recording, or by any information storage and retrieval system, without permission in writing from the publisher.

ISBN: 9781542655392
eBook ISBN: 9781732934511

Published by Hendricks Institute Publishing
226 W. Ojai Ave.
Suite 101, PMB 505
Ojai, CA 93023

DEDICATION

We dedicate this new edition of *The Corporate Mystic* to the remarkable executives, now numbering well more than a thousand, with whom we have consulted over the past five decades. These men and women have shown us the powerful truth of Kahlil Gibran's famous observation: *Work is love made visible.*

CONTENTS

ACKNOWLEDGMENTS

PROLOGUE
Heart and Soul at Work

INTRODUCTION
How to Recognize a Corporate Mystic:
Twelve Characteristics of Twenty-First-Century Leaders

PART ONE
The Mystic as Leader:
Becoming the Source

CHAPTER 1
Integrity:
Leadership by Inspiring Authenticity

♦ *What Integrity Actually Is* ♦ *Integrity Increases Vitality* ♦ *The Three Places to Look for Integrity Problems* ♦ *Taking Healthy Responsibility* ♦ *A New Definition of Responsibility* ♦ *How to Make and Keep Agreements* ♦ *How to Change an Agreement That Isn't Working* ♦ *Integrity Is a Matter of Physics as Much as Morality* ♦ *Standing on One Leg: How Non-Mystics Handle an Integrity Problem* ♦ *How Mystics Handle an Integrity Problem* ♦ *High-Firing as a Step to Integrity* ♦ *The Ultimate Payoff*

CHAPTER 2
Vision:
Leadership by Inspiring Clear Intention

♦ What Is Intention? ♦ How to Create a Powerful Intention ♦ Beware of Covert Intentions ♦ The Intention of Wholeness ♦ The Intention of Balance ♦ The Intention of Gratitude ♦ The Tyranny of Is ♦ The Tyranny of Because ♦ The Zone of Complacency ♦ What Do I Want? ♦ Developing No-Limits Vision ♦ Step Outside the Box ♦ Dealing with Idea-Slayers ♦ Future-Vision

CHAPTER 3
Intuition:
Leadership by Calling Forth Full Potential

♦ Intuition Plus Logic: The Corporate Mystic's Winning Formula ♦ Your Creative Think-Time Is Your Most Important Daily Business Activity ♦ Getting a Better Intuitive Hit Rate ♦ Becoming Bigger than the Problem ♦ Developing Good People-Intuition ♦ Intuitive Hiring ♦ Fear Clouds Intuition ♦ Removing the Inner Critic ♦ What We Fear Is Our Own Power ♦ Intuition Is a Phenomenon of the Gap ♦ Control Cramps Intuition ♦ Three Million Dollars' Worth of Intuition

PART TWO
The Practical Mystic:
Spirited Solutions to Everyday Business Problems

CHAPTER 4
Inspiring Commitment

♦ Recognizing the Most Common Commitment Problem ♦ Knowing Your Purpose ♦ The Purpose of Purpose ♦ Integrity Is Central to Commitment ♦ Doing What Needs to Be Done ♦ Why People Don't Honor Their

Commitments ♦ *Handling Fear, Doubt, and Confusion* ♦ *Misplaced Loyalties*
♦ *Recognizing and Rewarding Committed People*

CHAPTER 5
Communicating with People

♦ *Being Authentic* ♦ *Plain Talking* ♦ *Get Out of the Middle* ♦
Listening for Accuracy ♦ *Listening for Empathy* ♦ *Listening for Mutual Creativity* ♦ *Giving and Receiving Honest Feedback* ♦
Building a Corporate Culture of Integrity

CHAPTER 6
Managing Projects

♦ *Handling Big Wins and Big Losses* ♦ *Getting the Responsibility Formula Right* ♦ *Real Power* ♦ *Retaining High-Potential Employees* ♦ *Using Intuition to Avoid a Costly Mistake* ♦ *Handling Complainers and Low Producers* ♦ *How to Handle an Office Affair* ♦ *Ending Turf Battles* ♦
How to Keep Meetings from Being Boring ♦
Turning Adverse Situations into Breakthroughs

CHAPTER 7
Creating Wealth

♦ *Enlightened Perseverance* ♦ *Having What You Want* ♦ *Enjoying What You Have* ♦ *The Fundamental Law of Creating Wealth* ♦ *How to Create a Mind-Set of Prosperity in Your Organization* ♦ *Turning Around Negative Financial Attitudes* ♦ *Clean Up Your Unfinished Financial Business* ♦ *Leading with Gratitude* ♦ *Facing Your Internal Enemies of Abundance* ♦
Is Your Success a Burden? ♦ *Doing What You Love* ♦
Pulling the Plug on Drain-Relationships

PART THREE

The Disciplined Mystic
Four Ten-Minute Practices for Enhancing
Integrity, Vision, and Intuition

♦ *The Basic Centering Practice*
♦ *Your Integrity Worksheet: The F•A•C•T Process*
♦ *Future-Vision* ♦ *The Intuition Practice*

The Last Word

The Seven Radical Rules for Business Success

About the Authors

ACKNOWLEDGMENTS

We are deeply grateful to the following men and women for embodying the Corporate Mystic ideal and for enriching the lives of so many thousands of people in the process. An exhaustive list of the people we have admired, interviewed, followed around, or consulted with would fill a separate book. Forgive us if your name does not appear on this list, and know that your contribution is appreciated.

Brian Sharples, Founder and CEO, HomeAway
Tony Hsieh, CEO Zappos
Janet Mountain, Director, Michael and Susan Dell Foundation
Michael Dell, Founder and CEO, Dell Technologies
Mike Moritz, Chairman, Sequoia Capital
Annette Clayton, CEO and President, Schneider Electric North America
Bruce Gewertz, MD, Chairman of Surgery, Cedars Sinai Medical Center
Rob Kalin, Founder, Etsy
Larry Boucher, CEO, Auspex
Ron Bynum, corporate consultant
Kenneth Casey, President, Professional Investors' Financial Services
Paul and Elizabeth Cotulla, entrepreneurs
Stephen R. Covey, author and consultant
Carlene Ellis, Vice-President, Intel
Bob Galvin, Former Chairman, Motorola
Heath Herber, president, The Herber Company
Portia Isaacson, founder, Future Computing
Les Isbrandt, Vice-President, Warner Lambert
Kathryn Johnson, CEO, The Healthcare Forum
Jerry Jones, President, The Jones Corporation
Bill Kimpton, Founder and Chairman, Kimco
Philip Knight, Chairman, Nike

Barbara LaTour, Corporate Vice-President, Adecco
Kathy Mankin, Executive Vice-President, Heller Financial
Ed McCracken, CEO, Silicon Graphics
Richard McNeese, former CEO, First National Bancorp
Joyce Russell, President, Adecco Staffing USA
Ken Schroeder, CEO, KLA-Tencor
Jack Unroe, President, Judicial Arbitration and Mediation Services

*You must have a room,
or a certain hour or so a day, where you don't know
what was in the newspaper that morning,
you don't know who your friends are,
you don't know what you owe anybody,
you don't know what anybody owes you.
This is a place where you can simply experience and
bring forth what you are and what you might be.*

—JOSEPH CAMPBELL

*Often people attempt to live their lives backwards;
they try to have more things, or more money, in order
to do more of what they want, so they will be happier.
The way it actually works is in reverse. You must first
be who you really are, then do what you need to do, in
order to have what you want.*

—MARGARET YOUNG

PROLOGUE

HEART AND SOUL AT WORK

Work can provide the opportunity for spiritual and personal, as well as financial growth. If it doesn't, we're wasting far too much of our lives on it.

—JAMES AUTRY

Corporations are full of mystics. If you want to find a genuine mystic, you are more likely to find one in a boardroom than in a monastery or a cathedral. Surprised by this notion? We were, too. But over the past twenty-five years we have been in many boardrooms and many cathedrals, and we have discovered that the very best kind of mystics—those who practice what they preach—can be found in the business world. We are now convinced that the qualities of these remarkable people, and the principles they live by, will be the guiding force for twenty-first-century enterprise.

In preparation for writing this book, we spent a thousand hours in conversation with several hundred Corporate Mystics. As a result, our business and personal lives are forever changed. We will share with you the practical details of what they taught us: how to do soul-satisfying work in a way that empowers, heals, and profits. We have distilled their learnings into brief bits of "just-in-time" wisdom that you can draw on to help you in every minute of your work life.

We are consultants to corporations and to other corporate consultants. From working with eight hundred executives over the past twenty-five years, we make a prediction: Successful corporate leaders of the twenty-first century will be spiritual leaders. They will be comfortable with their own spirituality, and they will know how to nurture spiritual development in others. The most successful leaders of today have already learned this secret. Corporate Mystics know that an organization is a collective embodiment of spirit, the sum total of the spirits of the individuals who work there. Those who think spirituality has no place in business are selling themselves and those around them short.

What is a Corporate Mystic? The dictionary says that mystics are those who have been initiated into esoteric mysteries. It says that mystics intuitively comprehend what is true. The people we call Corporate Mystics seem to operate at a level of effectiveness that appears esoteric until you understand the principles they are drawing on. In addition, the mystics we have known definitely have a strong connection with their intuition and know how to use it where it counts. We go further in our definition, however: Corporate Mystics are those who operate from a base of integrity, pursue their visions with passion and compassion, and evoke the full potential of those with whom they come in contact.

Genuine Corporate Mystics live life from a spiritual base. They are in business for their hearts and souls as well as their wallets. They are in business to support the hearts and souls of the people with whom they work. We have done consulting work with many different types of organizations, so we have a basis for comparison when we say: There is more careful and conscious application of the Golden Rule in business settings than in any other institutions we have visited, including church, university, and government.

> *The key ingredient in strong relationships is to develop emotional connections. It's important to always act with integrity in your relationships, to be compassionate, friendly, loyal, and to make sure that you do the right thing and treat your relationships well.*
>
> —Tony Hsieh,
> CEO Zappos

Many of us have a deep sense of spiritual connection when we are young, only to have it erode as we enter the bottom-line world of adulthood. Childhood photographs often show us feeling wonder and delight. It looks as if we are spiritual beings having a physical experience. By adulthood we often look very different, like physical beings having, if we're fortunate, an occasional spiritual experience. The people we call Corporate Mystics have managed, through good fortune and diligence, to maintain their connection with the spiritual nature of themselves, other people, and the world around them.

A Corporate Mystic we interviewed for this book shared a story with us: "In my late thirties I felt like I was dying. I had been working in the corporate world for ten years, and though I had experienced quite a bit of success, I somehow knew I would never go all the way to the top. My office was on the tenth floor of a twenty-some-story building, and I remember looking out the window thinking that this was the story of my life. I was stuck on the tenth floor, halfway to the top. As I looked out the window I asked myself why this was true. After all, I worked hard and seemed as smart as everybody else. Then it hit me: I was split in half. Outside of work I was one way, but at work I was trying to be another person entirely. Outside work I was fascinated with human behavior and spent hours browsing in the psychology sections of bookstores. At work, though, I pretended to be this hard-driving fire engine of a person who was single-mindedly focused on numbers and productivity. I had the thought, 'The split is over; the way I am is the way I am, wherever I am.' I actually felt something shift in my body, like I was coming back together again. Looking back, I think what I was doing was accepting both halves of myself and making a bigger container for me to be all of myself. Now, as CEO, I try to emphasize a message of being your full, undivided self whenever I talk to the younger people in the company." This is an example of a spiritual awakening that had profound implications for this person's life and career.

When we talk about spirituality in business, we are talking about experiences, not religious beliefs. Religion usually refers to the organized aspects of spirituality: the rules, beliefs, and traditions that shape how spirituality shows up in the world. The Corporate Mystic demonstrates a type of spirituality that lives in deeds, not words. The Corporate Mystic is primarily interested in the benefits of spirituality, not in beliefs about it.

Corporate Mystics move easily between the spiritual world and the world of commerce. Corporate Mystics are visionaries with their feet on the ground.

They celebrate the oneness of everything, yet at the same time they are able to focus on details. They look at a mountain peak and a spreadsheet with the same eyes. They treat the janitor and their biggest client with the same attitude.

What follows is the distilled voice of our own learnings, influenced by the wisest men and women we have ever known. The Corporate Mystic is the mentor of our dreams, the voice that we wish had been coaching us through the tough times of life and business.

There is a Zen monastery near Tokyo that attracts many powerful executives from the nearby industrial cities. One day the master said: "There is no room in my monastery for mushy mystics, dreamy folks who leave their dirty teacups everywhere. Here we meditate and we wash our teacups. Both are equally important. We teach our students to be ruthlessly demanding of themselves and their colleagues. Expect the best! If people cannot function with clarity in the often-tough real world, their meditations and practices have been for naught. You must master two realities: You must revel in that vast inner space, the emptiness that is connected to all the emptiness everywhere. And at the very same time, you must give your full attention to the present moment, whether you are buying a train ticket or kissing your wife or reading the stock quotes."

We offer this book with respect to the hidden saints and mystics of the business world. May this wisdom enliven and enlighten all your hours, at work and at play.

INTRODUCTION

HOW TO RECOGNIZE A CORPORATE MYSTIC:

Twelve Characteristics of Twenty-First-Century Leaders

*The less effort,
the faster and more powerful you will be.*

—BRUCE LEE

Corporate Mystics have certain identifying characteristics. In this introduction, we will describe those characteristics as they appear from the outside. Then, in the rest of the book, we will show you the specific attitudes and action steps that will help you adopt these winning strategies for yourself.

We believe that these qualities will become crucial in the century to come, when change occurs at a rate that may be hard to imagine even in our speeded-up present. Here is an opportunity to check yourself out against these qualities, attitudes, and operating strategies. Find out how many of these characteristics are part of your life already.

In describing these traits let's make it clear that Corporate Mystics are perfectly human and therefore full of imperfections. These are street saints, front-line visionaries who have a hundred opportunities to mess up each day. They would be the last to say they have mastered the following traits. But we have seen with our own eyes that they are all in a serious inquiry into these characteristics every day they live and breathe.

ABSOLUTE HONESTY

Every single mystic we interviewed said the same thing: The first secret to success in business is to say only things that are true and to say them with total consistency. Businesspeople get into trouble when they say one thing to the banker, one thing to the customer, one thing to the board. We have facilitated many emotionally charged sessions in which company executives admitted lies, distortions, and concealments to people who had believed them. Yet even though these meetings were often loud and long, we have never seen a situation where absolute honesty did not pay off. People cannot relax and produce at their finest in an atmosphere of distortion and concealment. Honesty brings out the best in everyone. In other words, integrity is not just a noble idea, it's a tool for personal and corporate success.

Corporate Mystics are also honest, even brutally honest, with themselves. They want to know the truth, even though that truth sometimes is personally painful. In his first major consulting job, Gay had the sweaty task of delivering a litany of bad news to the president of the world's largest corporation of its kind. Not only was the news bad, but it involved one of the president's own pet projects. "I had been engaged to measure the success of the project and instead had found that practically everything was wrong with it," he recalls. "I went into the session feeling fear and trepidation. After all, I was a freshly minted psychologist, barely thirty years old, and he was a multimillionaire who frequently dined at the White House. I was worried that I would get blasted if I told him what I had concluded, but I decided to call it as I saw it. I had learned the hard way the consequences of soft-pedaling the truth, and I figured the worst he could do was fire me. But I soon found I had nothing to fear. When his attention focused on me I was treated to the best listening I had ever experienced. His interest did not waver, even during times I was telling him things he could not have possibly wanted to hear. There was never a trace of blame in his voice, either. His first move, upon hearing the bad news, was to reflect on whether anything was amiss in his own intentions and visions. He did this with the same attitude of blameless inquiry that he focused on the staff of the project under consideration. His attitude was: What actually happened? What can be done? Fix it or fold it? I had walked into the meeting expecting to be grilled and possibly dismissed from my contract. I walked out feeling completely valued. It was the first time in my life I was certain I had been in the presence of greatness."

There is no better catalyst to success than curiosity.

—MICHAEL DELL,
CEO AND CHAIRMAN, DELL TECHNOLOGIES

FAIRNESS

Scrupulous attention to fairness distinguishes the Corporate Mystic. They do what they say they are going to do. They don't do what they say they're not going to do. And all of this is carried out with across-the-board fairness and consistency. A high compliment often applied to the mystic is "Tough as nails but always fair." Everyone wants to be treated fairly, but many of us forget this under the stress of decision making. One of the mystic's edges is the ability to apply the question—Is it fair to all concerned?—even when the pressure is fully on.

For the Corporate Mystic, fairness goes beyond a moral injunction. In other words, they are not fair because they should be fair. They are fair because they see that equality pervades the universe. All of us are equal, all of us at the core are the same. As one person put it, "Fairness is the way everything hangs together in the world. When I act unfairly I disturb the actual workings of the world. When I am fair I participate in the way the world is woven together."

When Ken Levy of KLA Instruments was leading his firm through a tough time, he opened a meeting like this: "I'm announcing today across-the-board pay cuts of 10 percent for officers. Because I make more money than a lot of people in the company, I'm taking a 20 percent cut." People at the meeting, instead of grousing about their own cuts, tried to talk him down to 10 percent. He held firm, and the corporate grapevine hummed with this radical approach to fairness. Morale soared instead of plummeted.

SELF KNOWLEDGE

Human beings are born learning, and the moment we stop learning we start to die. Corporate Mystics are particularly concerned with learning about themselves. They recognize that our minds, bodies, and spirits are the instrument by which we carry out our actions, so they put a great deal of attention on examining their motives, history, and feelings.

Corporate Mystics are committed to their own learning and at the same time committed to helping others learn. The attitude of inquiry, of wonder, is sacred to the mystic. Few things anger them more than people claiming to be right, to have all the answers. We have not yet met a truly successful person who wasn't actively learning about themselves every day.

It's what you learn after you know it all that counts.

—JOHN WOODEN

As consultants, we are most often hired by an executive to work with his or her colleagues. A chairman will hire us to work with the company president, or the president may hire us to work with a management team. We can think of fewer than a dozen instances in which executives have sought our services for their own development. Yet in each case, they were extraordinary. Among them: The head of an entertainment conglomerate, a woman who is on her way to becoming the head of a *Fortune* 100 company, the chairman of a $20 billion company, a high-tech start-up entrepreneur. Our conclusion: The more talented you are, the more likely you are to go out of your way to learn and improve, even if you are phenomenally successful by the world's standards.

Corporate Mystics gain self-knowledge in three crucial ways. First, they acknowledge and appreciate their emotions. Although businesspeople have the reputation of being controlled and unemotional, and some certainly are, we have not found this to be true of the leaders we call mystics. More often, they simply deal with their feelings without dramatizing them. Mystics never hide their feelings, even their painful fears, angers, and griefs; they can report them to you with the same clarity as they can tell you the time of day.

Second, they understand their programming from the past, and hence are less likely to be blindsided by it. The mystics' edge is a thorough and deep knowledge of their own story—its limitations and glories—so that those limitations do not hold them back or overshadow the present.

Third, they are open to feedback, even when it is expressed as criticism. Kate was once invited to spend an evening working with the CEO and executives of a high-profile Silicon Valley company which is responsible for many innovations, including special effects for many hit Hollywood movies. The CEO met every month or two with the executive team for an evening of leading-edge learning. On this occasion, the focus was on getting feedback from people you worked closely with.

Kate: "I gave out colored sheets of paper, one color per person. I invited them to pick one area that needed improvement in themselves and in each of the other people present. Each person wrote his or her own area of improvement on a colored sheet, and peers used that color to select an area they felt that person needed to improve. Thus, every person gave themselves feedback, got feedback from the others, and gave the others feedback. It was a very rich evening of learning for all concerned, but two aspects stand out vividly in my memory. First, nearly every person picked out areas they needed to improve which were considered by the others to be strengths already. In other words, they were harder on themselves than the others were on them. Second, everyone was eager for the feedback! Nobody got defensive throughout the whole evening. I had done this activity with groups of middle managers at other companies and had seen a great deal of peevishness, put-downs, and general defensiveness. But the company had built a corporate culture of openness to personal learning. It was heartening to see a roomful of powerful executives who had such a high commitment to self-knowledge."

> *The trouble with most of us is that*
> *we would rather be ruined by praise*
> *than saved by criticism.*
>
> —NORMAN VINCENT PEALE

A FOCUS ON CONTRIBUTION

Jokesters and cartoonists often depict business leaders as greedy, but we have very seldom met a high-level leader who was motivated by greed. Most were deeply concerned with the well-being and empowerment of other people. Contribution was at the forefront of their intentions.

Early in his executive development work, one of Gay's clients was a CEO who had been uprooted by the shifting winds of corporate politics. Gay recalls, "I asked him point-blank why he didn't just retire right then in his early fifties. After all, I said, you have more than enough money to live on for the rest of your life. You could play golf, enjoy your grandchildren, get to know your wife. What would you miss that would be worth getting back into the fray for? He looked at me with a total incomprehension. '*The contribution*,' he explained, as if he were showing a child how a clock worked. 'When I retire I want to be completely satisfied that I have made my full contribution. I'm not finished yet.'

"At that moment I realized that I had never fully understood why people work. They work for contribution, for the opportunity to serve. Ultimately they work for love. I felt as if I were looking directly into his soul, into his deepest and highest motivation. This conversation allowed me to open up more to my own soul-level commitment to contribution."

NONDOGMATIC SPIRITUALITY

The four characteristics we have described—honesty, fairness, commitment to self-knowledge, and focus on contribution—are in themselves the ground of a perennial, universal spirituality. Corporate Mystics tend to be allergic to dogma, and often remain at a distance from religion in its more structured forms. Rather, they attempt to live their lives from the universal sources of spirituality that underlie differing beliefs. Bob Galvin once said that it is important for businesspeople to stay out of theology and potentially divisive beliefs about spirituality, and instead to focus on the unifying benefits of spiritual practice.

Above all; spirituality means deeds, not words, to the Corporate Mystic. They have an ability to see through the particulars to the universal connection points of us all. This ability to look beneath differences to the essential core frees up the mystic to focus on how spirituality expresses itself in action.

> *Spirituality cannot be something a person toys with,*
> *a little compartment of their lives.*
> *It has to be at the core,*
> *in a way that affects every other part of their lives.*
>
> —STEPHEN COVEY

> *My objective in life is not to have a spiritual part of*
> *life that is separate from the rest of my life.*
>
> —ED MCCRACKEN,
> CEO, SILICON GRAPHICS

THEY GET MORE DONE BY DOING LESS

An executive of a West Coast corporation describes his first morning as an aide to his mentor many years before. "He had an apartment in the corporate headquarters, and that's where I was asked to meet him that first morning. He came out of the door at seven A.M., greeted me, and took me into his office with him. An hour later, I excused myself to go to the bathroom. When I got in there, I just stood there shaking and trying to catch my breath. He had gotten more done in an hour than I had ever done in two weeks! And yet he did it all effortlessly; one thing just flowed into another. He never even looked like he was working. He focused all his attention on what he was doing right then and there, then he went to the next thing and gave it that same attention. It was remarkable to see someone so centered in the present. I felt like a U-Haul trailer being pulled along behind a Ferrari. I vowed then and there that if I ever found myself working too hard or looking busy, I would take it as a sign that I wasn't working smart."

> Man: I'm a hard-driving businessman. If I learn to meditate, won't it take the drive out of me?
> Zen master: No, no. It will simply make you an easy-driving businessman. Whoever said the drive had to be hard?

To get more done by doing less is a credo and a key operating style of Corporate Mystics. They put a great deal of attention on learning to be in the present because they have found that this is the only place from which time can be expanded. If you are in the present—not caught up in regret about the past or anxiety about the future—time essentially becomes malleable. When you are in the grip of the past or the future, there is never enough time, because you are trying to be in two places at once. If you are standing in the present while your mind is somewhere else, there is a fundamental split that produces pressure and tension. Only by coming into the present can the mystic master time. Corporate Mystics study carefully how time feels to them. When time pressures begin to creep in, they use this as feedback that they are not centering themselves in the present.

> *Move like a beam of light,*
> *Fly like lightning,*
> *Strike like thunder,*
> *Whirl in circles around a stable center.*
>
> —MORIHEI UESHIBA

THEY CALL FORTH THE BEST OF THEMSELVES AND OTHERS

Most mystical traditions speak of a clear space at the center of ourselves, whether it is called soul or spirit or essence. It is what some call the higher self and represents who we really are at the core. Corporate Mystics know how to stay focused on this essence in themselves and in their co-workers, and how to bring it forth reliably.

> *At every moment you choose yourself but do you choose your self? Body and soul contain a thousand possibilities out of which you may build many "I's." But in only one of them is there congruence between the elector and the elected, only one which you will never find until you have excluded all those superficial feelings and possibilities of being and doing with which you toy out of curiosity or wonder or fear and which hinder you from casting anchor in the experience in the mystery of life and the consciousness of the talent entrusted in you and the wonder of you which is truly your "I."*
>
> —DAG HAMMARSKJÖLD

Essence is distinct from persona. Persona, coming from a word that means "mask," is the act we wear to survive in the world. You may have learned the persona of "appeaser" or "dominator" to survive in your particular family, and you may still run that act in your workplace today. Mystics know that we all have personas that are wrapped around our true essence, but they also know that we are not our personas. They know that underneath the blustery facade of the tough supersalesman may be a terrified little boy. But the boy, too, is a persona, and both may obscure the true self of the person beneath all the masks. The true self is often characterized by wonder, curiosity, and openness to resonance with others, qualities that often become obscured in the growing-up process. Once we become fully identified with our essence, we feel at home wherever we are.

Corporate Mystics develop a kind of double vision, at once able to see the mask and the essential person inside.

This skill has a high payoff in confronting difficult people. Because Corporate Mystics see and honor the person's essence, they can say things like "You can be a total jerk sometimes, Harry," and have it meaningfully received. Without respect of the person's essence, the same comment triggers resistance. Kate recalls the breakthrough moment of an executive development session with Linda Smith, a senior vice-president of a multinational company: "With no malice intended, I referred to her as a 'political boob.' She got to laughing so hard at this description of her that tears poured down her face. I think I could get away with saying something like this because I could see her essence—her pure nature—so clearly, and because she knew her own essence-nature so deeply. Hearing this feedback from someone who saw her essence deeply triggered an important behavioral shift in her toward increased political astuteness."

It is as important to challenge people about their personas as it is to love and cherish their true essence. In the business world it is dangerous to ignore people's personas. Genuinely caring for people means seeing them as they are, not blithely overlooking possibly fatal flaws.

OPENNESS TO CHANGE

Mystics have a respect and even a fondness for change that reaches down into their cells. They know that everything is change—that's the way life works in this part of the universe. As one Corporate Mystic put it: Everything in the universe is subject to change and everything is right on schedule. At times they may have unpleasant feelings about the direction of change, but they are careful not to let those feelings limit their ability to respond.

One of the major talents Corporate Mystics develop is the ability to let go of being right. Attachment to one's own point of view is a make-or-break problem for many people because it blinds them to the need for change. In the course of our work with over eight hundred executives, we have invited twelve thousand of their co-workers to fill out surveys rating their performance. One survey item asks if the executive is willing to let go of no-win situations or goals. The responses indicate that this is a problem for about 50 percent of the executives.

> *Depending on the circumstances,*
> *You should be hard as a diamond,*
> *Flexible as a willow,*
> *Smooth-flowing like water*
> *or as empty as space.*
>
> —Morihei Ueshiba

Gay has traded commodity and stock index futures for many years. He has learned the hard way about letting go. "If I buy a contract for a thousand barrels of oil at $20 a barrel, I have reason to believe that it will go up. If it goes down to $18 a barrel an hour after I buy it, I am faced with a dilemma. Sell out now and take a $2,000 loss, or hold it and hope it comes back up? If I hold on, it could keep going on down. This nerve-wracking moment is the one that keeps most people out of the game, but I have learned to savor it. It comes down to admitting you're wrong. The winner will say: 'Okay, I'm wrong. It's going down. I'll get out, take my loss, and maybe sell a contract instead of buying one.' In other words, winners play it the way it's going. Losers say: 'I know I'm right, darn it, even though the market says otherwise. I'll just stay in a little longer and I'm sure I'll be proven right.' Some truly colossal disasters have come from thinking this way."

When Coca-Cola changed the formula of their flagship product some years ago, there was a large hue and cry from their loyal customers who liked the old formula. Apparently there was a faction of executives within the company who wanted to stick with the new formula and ride out the uproar. Another faction took the "go with the flow" approach and voted to bring back the old formula. The second group prevailed, indicating that the company would rather listen to the customer than be right. Corporate Mystics learn to flow with change and even thrive on it. The non-mystic gets seasick amid change by trying to pretend he's still on dry land.

> *We must all learn not only to not fear change,*
> *but to embrace it enthusiastically, and*
> *perhaps even more important,*
> *to encourage and drive it enthusiastically.*
>
> —Tony Hsieh,
> CEO Zappos

A SPECIAL SENSE OF HUMOR

Corporate Mystics laugh a lot. They are quick to point out the quirks of life and the human animal, and they are quick to include themselves in the joke. They can laugh at themselves and do because they have embodied a basic duality: the sacredness of life and the utter absurdity of it at times. Kate, who has observed dozens of corporate cultures, says, "The single best way to judge the health of a team or a company is by how much humor there is."

In our five decades in the presence of corporate leaders, we have seldom heard jokes or remarks that relied upon cruelty, humiliation, or ridicule for their humor. This in itself is remarkable, but it gives an insight into the viewpoint of the mystic: We are all in this together—let's laugh ourselves out of this fix we're in.

KEEN DISTANT VISION AND UP-CLOSE FOCUS

Corporate Mystics have a gift for engaging people in big dreams. They can stand in a future that does not exist and map out the details of how to get there. (We will tell you exactly how they do this in a later chapter.) At the same time they can look steadily at right-now reality. Many people have a grasp of the nuts-and-bolts reality of the moment. They can look at the way things are and not flinch. On the other end of the spectrum, there are also people who can see the possibilities on the horizon. But often these two skills—keen distant vision and equally keen up-close focus—do not come in the same package. In Corporate Mystics, they do. One of the striking characteristics of the mystics we've met is their comfort with this twofold vision.

Twofold vision also includes the ability to focus on the separateness and the way everything is woven together. People at the top of companies have a feeling for the wholeness of the organization, the people in it and the way it all fits together. Decisions made from this sense of wholeness tend to be sound and fair. One observation we have made is that there is more ecological awareness at the top of companies than the casual observer might suspect. News reports of, say, the logging industry tend to play up the "bottom-line" mentality of corporate leaders in contrast to the "natural" concerns of eco-activists. But, like most gross generalizations, these obscure the truth. Contrary to public opinion, business leaders tend to be quite mindful of the big picture. It is just that the big picture for them includes the families of the people who work for the company in addition to the aspects of nature with which the company is in conflict.

The head of a Rocky Mountain communication company reminisced about the first time he saw this quality: "My high school football team was coached by a fine man named Coach Ford. Sometimes he would call me over to give me some bit of individual coaching. All the while he was talking to me, his eyes would be sweeping the field where the rest of the team was practicing. He had the skill of carrying out a detailed conversation with one person while covering the whole scene in his vision. I couldn't have put it in words at the time, but what I was learning from him was how to stay firmly in the present and in my vision of how the future could be, all at the same time."

During an interview over lunch for this book, a client interrupted a visionary discourse about twenty-first-century business to point out something we hadn't noticed. The waiter was setting up for dinner in another section of the restaurant, and our (long overstayed) presence was getting in his way. This is an example of the twofold vision of the Corporate Mystic: to be concerned simultaneously about the visionary future and how to make someone's life easier right this minute.

The Corporate Mystic carries this respect into other dimensions. They cultivate an ability to live in multiple "time zones," with a respect for past, present, and future all at once. It is a kind of moving-average approach to life in which past, present, and future are all factored into the equation. Those who get far out in the future often underestimate the time and resources necessary to get there. Those who are stuck in the past cannot meet the present or the future effectively. It takes a keen grasp of the present situation, a respect for the past, and a sense of the future to work effectively in this current age of sweeping and rapid change.

Mystics can enroll and engage others in their vision of what is possible, even though these visions at first seem like "impossible dreams." John Kennedy, at his inauguration in 1961, not only described the impossible dream of putting a man on the moon. He seemed effortlessly to enroll everyone else in it as well. A few people said it was a kooky, expensive idea, but nearly everyone got on board. This feat was a classic example of the mystic at work.

AN UNUSUAL SELF-DISCIPLINE

Corporate Mystics are fiercely disciplined, but it is a discipline born of passion. They generally do not rely on the kind of authoritarian discipline that is driven by fear. They motivate themselves through a clear sense of purpose, not with the shoulds and oughts of a fantasized ideal. This type of discipline makes them flexible and adaptable rather than rigid.

Corporate Mystics are passionate people. They play to win, of course, but more importantly, they play to play. We have had the opportunity to go from boardroom to golf course to family dinner with many mystics, and have been deeply impressed with their ability to be passionately present in each situation. Ken Casey, head of Professional Investors' Financial Services, is one of the most passionate participants in life we've met. Ken said: "I retired in my early forties with the vision of having plenty of time to run on the beach with my dog. After running on the beach with my dog for two or three days, I sat down to rest and wondered—'Is this it?' I realized I loved what I'd been doing, so I went back and stepped back into leadership again." But that's not all. As we got to know him, we found that he spends considerable time raising money for a home for abused children. Then we found out that he also sings in the chorus in an opera company. Then we discovered that he is one of the top whitewater rafters in the world. One of his latest exploits was to open up the Upper Zambezi to rafters for the first time, during which his team was attacked by crocodiles between sixty and seventy times! He is also a world-class soccer player. This is clearly a person who plays passionately in every area of life.

To play with passion requires discipline. There is no other way to generate the tireless source of energy that passion runs on. You set high standards and you hold to them. The act of making good on your commitments to yourself and others is what generates the high level of energy needed to run a successful life.

> *Obsessives, those who cannot imagine doing anything else with their lives, always find their work more fulfilling than those who find themselves in a profession because it was expected of them or because they did not have a calling that tugged at their emotions. For those who are obsessed by a pursuit, there is no separation between life and work,...making it much easier to endure all the setbacks, reversals and frustrations...that come with entrepreneurship. Passion is necessary, but it's not enough.*
>
> —MIKE MORITZ,
> PARTNER, SEQUOIA CAPITAL
> LEGENDARY FOR HIS INVESTMENTS,
> BIGGEST HITS: GOOGLE, PAYPAL, ZAPPOS

BALANCE

Mystics keep a keen eye on balancing their lives in four main areas: intimacy (including marriage, family, and close friendship), work, spirituality, and community (including social and political life). The balance between work and intimacy is usually where problems occur. A considerable amount of our consultation time has gone into helping extremely busy people achieve a harmonious balance between work and home.

> *It is your work in life that is the ultimate seduction.*
>
> —PABLO PICASSO

Corporate Mystics strive for balance in each of the key areas of life. Many people mess up by trying to get their home needs met at work, and vice versa. A person who is hurting because he does not know how to communicate with his kids becomes a blustery communication obstructor at work. Another person walks in the door at night so full of undigested work issues that no one in the family can get through to her. This problem, unless corrected, becomes a self-fulfilling spiral downward. He or she spends more time at work to get away from home problems, which creates more conflict at home, which causes them to withdraw into work more.

Stephen Covey is one of the few major voices emphasizing the need for balance in order to achieve genuine success. One of the reasons for the enthusiastic reception of his books and seminars is a deep hunger for balance in the corporate world. In our consulting work, we often must deal with the fallout from imbalanced lives: problems with children, marital strains, psychosomatic illnesses. Part of the problem is time management, but more fundamentally it is a matter of commitment to balance. Logic and emotion, home and work, future and now: all of these can be sources of deep division, splits within ourselves that can destroy us. But with the proper commitment and some practice, they can also be sources of unity in the healed wholeness of ourselves. This is the territory that the mystic walks, not unfalteringly, but with commitment and passion.

"Master," said the student, "where do you get your spiritual power?"

"From being connected to the source," said the Master.

"You are connected to the source of Zen?"

"Beyond that," said the Master, "I am Zen. The connection is complete."

"But isn't it arrogant to claim connection with the source?" asked the student.

"Far from it," said the Master. "It's arrogant not to claim connection with the source. Everything is connected. If you think you are not connected to the source you are thumbing your nose at the universe itself."

PART ONE

THE MYSTIC AS LEADER: BECOMING THE SOURCE

> *When you walk with purpose, you collide with destiny.*
>
> —BERTRICE BERRY

If you will open up to being a source of integrity, vision, and intuition in your organization, you step into leadership regardless of what niche you occupy. Many people wait to be instructed or reminded to take full ownership of these powers. The Corporate Mystic knows that real power and real fun comes from being a source. When you are the source, you take full responsibility for bringing into being the corporate culture you want. Everyone can be the source, and when they think they are, they are.

If you are willing to let go of your resistance to being a source, you claim a type of spiritual power that others can feel.

Leaders are comfortable with being a source of integrity, vision, and intuition. They seek to be producers, not consumers of these three rare commodities. Inspired leaders, though, have something extra. They are committed to everyone else being a source. In other words, they are committed to being a source of sources. This takes them out of the power game. If you set yourself up as the source of something while disempowering those around you, look out. It may feel great for a while, but the costs are enormous. You risk playing Daddy or Mommy to people who are still looking for someone to take care of them. Boardrooms are not immune to this problem.

Imagine what could happen in your organization if everyone were trained to be a source of integrity. In a work space in which everyone felt connected to the source of integrity, miracles would happen every day. All the energy usually wasted on cleaning up integrity breaches could be channeled into creativity.

The same thing is true for vision or intuition. Imagine the power of an organization where everyone was empowered to be visionary. In our corporate training workshops we get to see this happen week after week, but it never fails to move us. A typical situation is that one person in a room of twenty will be the only one operating in the visionary role at the beginning of the workshop. Usually this is the CEO or highest officer; frequently it is the person who arranged for the training to take place. After three days of work, though, the picture is very different. All twenty are now taking responsibility for being the source of vision for the company. The energy in the room is humming with shared excitement. Everyone is on the same frequency because everyone is source.

Source is where the creativity comes from. It is also where the profits and the fun come from. People who connect with source get to inspire creativity, profits, and fun. Everybody else gets to sit on the bench and grouse. In this part we will explore how to go about becoming the source of integrity, vision, and intuition in your organization.

1

INTEGRITY:

LEADERSHIP BY INSPIRING AUTHENTICITY

*I'm sometimes too blunt, but it's most important to be
open and straightforward and tell the truth.
This helps with bureaucracy and turf battles:
As soon as you're open and listening and willing to
dialogue, people are remarkably receptive and changes
speed up rapidly.*

— A Corporate Mystic

Integrity creates a force field of aliveness, energy, and creativity around you. An integrity breach clouds the field around you, making creativity impossible. Lack of integrity leaches energy from you, your colleagues, and the company.

Taking a stand for integrity will create a stirring of energy throughout your organization. It will also create a stirring inside yourself. Committing yourself to integrity flushes to the surface any aspect of yourself and your organization that is not committed to integrity. The moment after you take a stand for integrity you might suddenly start thinking of some lie you told sixteen years ago. That's because your commitment to integrity is penetrating your body, flushing out anything in its way. The same thing happens in organizations. One person's stand for integrity will have a ripple effect. It will cause some people to move toward integrity, others to resist it. But the power of an integrity stand cannot be denied. You cannot ignore it.

The CEO of a Fortune 50 giant tells this story: "In the early 1950s we had the opportunity to get a huge contract with a South American country, installing a microwave radio system. The first part of the contract was for $10 million worth of work, which in the context of our overall revenues in excess of $100 million represented a very large possibility. One of the executives came in and told me that we had won the order but that he had decided not to take it. The reason: The generals who ran the country wanted the contract to read $11 million so they could skim the difference off the top. I told him that I was sorry that this had happened, and to refuse the contract even if they dropped their demand for padding and wanted to do it at the original price. Further, I told him that we would do no further business with this country until there was a change of leadership." When you take strong stands like this, people come to understand that you mean what you say. And the results speak for themselves: The generals are long gone, Motorola is still here.

There is a deeply personal and highly visible reason to focus on integrity: Your face will light up when you act with integrity or correct an integrity breach. Your mood will drop like a rock when you commit an integrity breach. If you are not feeling fully engaged throughout your workday, it's likely you've cut a deal somewhere that's robbing your energy.

When businesspeople stop and consider it, they are always shocked to discover how much time, energy, and money are wasted by integrity problems. But the positive flip side of this is also true: Creativity is unleashed by attending to integrity. If you feel like something isn't being said in a conversation, for example, stop right there and say so. If you are on the wrong track, you'll find out soon enough. But if you don't say something you will carry the incomplete interchange away with you. Then a small portion of your mind will still be occupied with it, the same small portion that you need for creative breakthroughs.

Integrity allows you to make an authentic connection with people, especially those you want to be close to. Without integrity, there is no relationship, only entanglement. The dictionary tells us that an *entanglement* is "two or more things enfolded upon each other so that the freedom of each is compromised." That's what happens when people fall out of integrity with each other.

Integrity is the great simplifier of life. As Henry David Thoreau said, the three things we all need to do to be happy is "simplify, simplify, simplify." As Gay's grandmother put it, "If you always tell the truth, you don't have to remember what you said." If you are a student of integrity, you don't have to waste thought, energy, or time looking for where the problem is. You know that when things aren't working to look at integrity.

Mystics know a secret: Integrity works. It is not just a noble idea, it is a crucial set of operating principles. It takes a great deal of energy to be out of integrity, to live in a state of separation from the wholeness of life. This wasted energy is a poisonous force for destruction in personal and corporate life. If we pretend that our actions have no consequences—if we think we can get away with anything at all in these speeded-up times—we are setting ourselves up for the rudest of awakenings.

Many people have never been members of an organization—be it a family, a club, or a company—that operated in a state of full integrity. We can tell you that the feeling is exhilarating. We have had the great pleasure of helping many organizations dig themselves out of pits caused by integrity breaches. Sometimes it has taken months—and even years—of hard work for them to go from a culture of nonintegrity to a culture of integrity. The results have been well worth it in every case we've seen.

In our travels in and around the corporate world, we have found that people are basically well intentioned. There will always be bad apples, but that's never the real problem. The problem is that people are unclear about just what integrity is. They don't know the navigational principles of integrity and how to make it work for them in the corporate environment. In this chapter, we endeavor to take some of the mystery out of integrity.

> *Character is what you are*
> *in the dark.*
>
> —DWIGHT L. MOODY

WHAT INTEGRITY ACTUALLY IS

The mastery of integrity comes down to three things: being authentic with yourself, being authentic with others, and doing the things you have said you would do.

If you will commit to this kind of authenticity, you have a chance to embrace the ultimate in integrity: owning your own soul and making it unsellable. By knowing yourself completely, you become immune to self-deception.

Honesty means full disclosure to myself and others, with good intent.

—Susan Scott

Before looking at these three areas, though, we need to confront something even more fundamental. Are you committed to your own full development and the success of the organization you're in?

Inside each of us there are two strong pulls. One pull is toward complete independence—becoming our own person through and through. But there is also a strong pull to commit ourselves in something larger: communion with other people, a company or family, the universe itself. Both pulls must be honored and developed fully. Some people are tugged too far in one direction and are thrown out of balance. One imbalance is to stay so independent that you never have the deep joy of surrendering yourself to something larger. Another imbalance is to surrender yourself so thoroughly that there's nobody home when you wake up one day and ask, "Who am I?" Corporations are full of people with each of these imbalances. There are those who hold back and never really surrender to full participation. And there are those who are swallowed up by the company so that they have no life of their own.

Corporate Mystics study this problem carefully, knowing that both strong pulls must be developed in themselves. They know that they must surrender fully to the team enterprise while at the same time being completely committed to themselves as separate individuals. Neither one commitment nor the other will do; both must be fully honored.

*When we create advertising from a place of
integrity—when we tell the truth about a product or
service dramatically in a way that doesn't seek to
motivate people to buy from a place of fear—
that advertising is the most successful
for both the client and the agency.*

—MARK HORN, VICE-PRESIDENT AND CREATIVE
SUPERVISOR, WUNDERMAN CATO JOHNSON

INTEGRITY INCREASES VITALITY

Integrity feels good. When you come from integrity, there will be a streamlining of resources throughout your body. Check it out for yourself. Next time you clear up an integrity breach—"Jim, I told you I would return your call at noon but I didn't get back to you until 1:30"—notice what happens in your body right afterward. Usually, you will feel an energetic sense of relaxed alertness. Suddenly you can bring all of your attention to bear on the moment. Because you pay attention to integrity, you have free energy that will amplify your power to accomplish whatever you want.

One mystic put it this way: "When I'm in integrity I feel full-contactedness with the world and with others. I can let go instead of holding myself. I feel an openness in my face and skin, a pleasant kind of fullness—the way I feel after I've taken a shower. I feel an activation in my body that is relaxed and alert. I feel curious and very calm. My intuition is heightened. I make leaps and see images more clearly. I listen better, because I'm not listening through a filter of 'Are they gonna get me?' I feel happy for no reason when I'm in integrity."

*The certain test of sanity
is if you accept life whole,
as it is.*

—Lao-Tzu

THE THREE PLACES TO LOOK FOR INTEGRITY PROBLEMS

Nearly every personal or corporate disaster begins with an integrity problem, and often a small one. Left untended, like a tiny shimmy in your front wheels, a small integrity problem can escalate quickly to shake loose anything that's not tightly connected. When things are not going well and you cannot figure out why, assume an integrity glitch. This is not because people are fundamentally bad but rather because true integrity is hard to master. Here are the three key questions to ask yourself:

Are you being authentic with yourself?
The first question to ask is whether you are out of integrity with yourself. Are you genuinely at ease with the path you are on? Many of us learn very early to tune out inner signals, and the long-run costs of this are enormous. We receive a signal that says "Don't do this," and then we go ahead and do it anyway. Nearly everyone we have talked to who was involved in large integrity breaches felt uncomfortable at the very beginning. They overrode that feeling and rationalized it away.

Being human, we often need a number of trials to get this lesson right. Even if you have been avoiding the subject, begin the learning process this minute. Pause right now and ask: Are there any places now in my life where I'm lying to myself? Happiness flows from a clear spring: You need to have a totally honest relationship with yourself.

Your feelings are a key part of the equation. There are three feelings you need to become comfortable with, so comfortable that you can talk about them calmly. These are fear, anger, and sadness. To be in integrity with your feelings, you must be able to know when you are scared, angry, and/or sad, and to be able to say "I'm scared" or "I'm angry" or "I'm sad." Many interpersonal problems come from hiding feelings from ourselves or each other. These can only be resolved by knowing ourselves intimately and being able to speak the truth of our emotions to each other.

Our bodies are where our feelings live, not our minds. Yet very little training is ever given in body awareness as we're growing up, so many of us have to start from scratch as adults. In a saner world, first-graders would be taught the difference between anger and fear, for example, and where those feelings live in their bodies. As adults, we often have a great deal of confusion about feelings. We get scared, perhaps, and instead of saying "I'm scared," we hide our fear and lash out in anger. We get angry and instead of saying "I'm angry," we burst into tears.

If we are out of integrity with ourselves—not knowing who we are, how we feel, what we want—it sets up a rattle that throws everything off. But when we take this rattle out into the world around us, real trouble, even dangerous trouble, begins to occur.

Are you being authentic with others?

The second question to ask is whether there are or have been any distortions in your communications to others. Bluntly put: Where are the lies in your life? If you find a lie, first acknowledge it to yourself: "I told Company X that Company Y was buying our brand of software. That was a lie, but I was scared I wouldn't make quota unless I made the sale." This step is essential; otherwise you throw your own system out of kilter. Next, square yourself with the relevant people. A ten-second communication is usually what it takes: "Jerry, I told you that Company Y was buying our software. The truth was that they hadn't bought it yet, but I wanted to sell you our software and I thought knowing Company Y was buying it would inspire you." The big fear, of course, is that your listener will get mad and punish you in some way. Trust will be destroyed (forgetting, of course, that we have already destroyed the trust). Occasionally it happens that way, but more often your listener will be grateful and trust will be enhanced in the long run.

Sigmund Freud was asked to summarize his life work in one sentence. He replied, "Secrets make you sick." Lies and secrets can make companies sick, too. There is no faster way to poison the community well than to stir lies into it. Of course, we are not talking about "healthy" secrets, such as the patent to a computer chip or the secret to the Coke formula. The kinds of lies and secrets that hurt companies usually involve withholding information—the president is having an affair with the vice-president—in order to protect someone.

> *There is no such thing as a minor lapse of integrity.*
>
> —TOM PETERS

Are you doing the things you said you'd do?

The third place to ask when things go wrong is whether you have broken any agreements. Often the agreement is tiny, the breach slight. But it isn't a matter of size. Look how much shimmy you get from a tiny front-end misalignment. The mystic knows that there is only one thing to be done when an agreement has been breached: Stand and face it. State it clearly: "Jim, I said I would have the report to you by 5:00 P.M. It's ten past now and it's coming off the printer. I regret any inconvenience." Then, pause and listen. Maybe the other person has a reaction, maybe it doesn't matter a whit. Winners cop to it and hear out any reaction. Losers are too busy with fancy footwork:

- making excuses,
- laying the blame elsewhere,
- promising to do better, and so on.

Corporate ditches all over the land are littered with habitual excuse makers.

> *I contend that dishonesty will create a failure force that often manifests itself in other ways—ways not apparent to the outside observer.*
>
> —JOSEPH SUGARMAN

TAKING HEALTHY RESPONSIBILITY

Integrity culminates in the ability to take full, effective responsibility. The ordinary definition of responsibility: Whose fault is this? The successful person's definition: How can I respond to this so that everybody wins?

All the best responsibility is taken. In other words, genuine responsibility—the kind that changes your life—does not begin until you actively take it. There is no magic age when you become responsible. Some people go to their graves avoiding responsibility. Corporate Mystics surf on the edge of responsibility, always asking themselves how they can take healthy responsibility for the issue at hand.

If your definition of responsibility focuses on fault and blame, you are pointed in three fruitless directions: It's their fault, it's my fault, it's the world's fault. None of these directions lead to effective action.

The mystic knows there are only two relevant questions: What can I learn from this? and What needs to be done? The first question opens you to infinity itself, because there is that much to learn from any situation, and the second question focuses you on the infinitely practical.

Responsibility is to keep the ability to respond.

—GUSTAV MAHLER

Here is an example of the power of responsibility. It shows how one person who steps into full responsibility inspires others to do the same. When these events took place, Ron Bynum was the leader of a training organization that used a former summer camp as one of its facilities. One night he was reading at home when his phone rang with dramatically bad news: One of the buildings at his training center had caught fire and burned down quickly. Someone had left a towel near a heater in a dormitory where some of the staff lived. The old wooden building had gone up in flames like a bundle of kindling.

When he got to the center the staff of nearly one hundred was in an uproar. Everybody, even the site manager, was in a tumult of blame and self-recrimination. Our mystic called a meeting in the main hall and took the stage. His words went like this:

"I want to raise the question of who is responsible for this situation." He paused as the group went into an uproar of finger-pointing. He waited for it to die down. "The answer is very clear to me," he said. "I'm responsible." Dead silence filled the room. "Wait a minute," someone said. "You weren't even here. How come you're responsible?"

"I'm responsible because I'm claiming responsibility. That's all that really matters. If you're looking for details, I've been in that dormitory a dozen times this summer, and I could have noticed that the towel rack was too close to the heater. But I didn't. So that's one reason I'm responsible. But the details are irrelevant. How about if we all take responsibility rather than blaming ourselves or somebody else? Then let's find out what needs to be done." The atmosphere in the room shifted in a second. Blame and recrimination stopped cold; the conversation turned to solutions. By stepping into responsibility, he got everybody heading in a productive direction. What more could be asked of a leader?

Problems begin to dissolve the moment someone steps into being a source. Leaders deserve to be leaders not because they are always the source of integrity but because they can step into it quickly when they see they have stepped out of integrity. In other words, Corporate Mystics are not saints who are above it all. Rather, they are nimble at seeing when an opportunity arises to claim their connection with the source.

> *There's never been a better time to change the way you think. Replace every 'I can't' with 'How can I?' It might sound like semantics, but I promise it will bring whatever you want to accomplish much closer to becoming a reality.*
>
> — MAYNARD WEBB,
> FOUNDER, WEBB INVESTMENT NETWORK
> AND FORMER COO OF EBAY

A NEW DEFINITION OF RESPONSIBILITY

Kathlyn Hendricks, corporate consultant (and Gay's wife), stands in front of a group of about twenty people, all top-level executives of one of America's largest companies. She holds a hundred-dollar bill aloft, then passes it around the room for all to touch. Even though all the people in the room make million-dollar decisions on a regular basis, and many of them are themselves millionaires, there is still something attention getting about a hundred-dollar bill. There are quizzical looks as the bill goes around.

She attaches the bill with a clip to an easel.

"Who is responsible for this bill being here?" she asks.

There is silence, punctuated by a few snickers. She repeats the question, carefully keeping the wording the same.

"You are," someone finally says.

"Why?" Kathlyn asks.

"It's obvious. Because you put it there," the person says.

"Okay, let's look at that," says Kathlyn. "One way we think about responsibility is 'Who did this?' Many of us first became acquainted with this question when Mom or Dad saw something amiss and said, 'Who's responsible for this?'"

There are chuckles around the room as people remember their experiences with this kind of responsibility.

Kathlyn writes on the easel, making two big columns. One column is entitled: Familiar Definitions of Responsibility. The other column is entitled: Breakthrough, Life-Changing Definition of Responsibility. She writes "Who did it?" under Familiar Definitions.

"We'll put it in that category because we're all familiar with it, and because knowing who did it does not often generate a creative breakthrough or change lives."

Kathlyn asks again. "Who's responsible for this hundred-dollar bill being here?"

Silence prevails, then someone says, "We all are."

"Why?" Kathlyn asks.

"Because most of us touched it when it went around. And even if you didn't touch, at least we all saw it."

"Let's look at that explanation," says Kathlyn. "When you think about it, though, this is an elaboration of the first definition we came up with. Instead of 'Who did it?' we have 'Who participated in the chain of events that led to things being the way they are?' This definition of responsibility gets a lot of press when things like Watergate or the Iran–Contra scandal happen. The president and whoever else can muster the power try to depict themselves as being out of the loop. Meanwhile the opposition tries to prove that the president was definitely in the loop. But, really, this is another way of saying 'Who did it?'" She writes "Who participated in the Chain of Events?" in the column entitled Familiar Definitions of Responsibility.

"Aha!" someone says. "The U.S. Treasury is really responsible."

"Why?" Kathlyn asks.

"They printed the bill," the person says. Many murmurs of agreement rustle around the room.

"Okay," Kathlyn says. "Let's look at it that way. Isn't that really an extension of the Familiar Paradigm? It's taking that paradigm to the source. The Treasury is responsible because they started the chain of events that led to things being the way they are." There are murmurs of assent, and she writes "Who started it?" in the Familiar Definitions column.

Now there are many frowns and crossed limbs in the room. They are, in a word, stumped.

Kathlyn lets them endure a long silence, allowing the creative tension to build.

Suddenly someone bolts upright.

"I'm responsible for it being there," the person says.

"Prove it," says Kathlyn.

He steps quickly to the front of the room and takes the hundred-dollar bill from the easel.

"I'm responsible because it's not there anymore. I took responsibility for changing it."

Kathlyn smiles. "He took responsibility for changing it. Regardless of who started it. Regardless of who touched it. Regardless of who participated in the chain of events. He stood up and did it. Congratulations. That's the breakthrough, life-changing definition of responsibility."

She leads applause for him. He goes over to her and tries to give her the bill back.

"Keep it," she says. "Responsibility has its rewards."

HOW TO MAKE AND KEEP AGREEMENTS

A simple definition of an agreement is anything you have said you would do, or anything you have said you would not do. Part of the art of successful living (and working) depends on learning how to make and keep your agreements.

If you say the report will be on someone's desk at 5:00 P.M., you have to have it there or agree to change the agreement. By making the agreement you have created a new entity in the universe. Before you created this entity there was no such thing as "The report being on Jim's desk at 5:00 P.M." By making this agreement you joined forces with the creative power in the universe, the same power that makes oak trees where no trees were before. Having stepped into unity with the creative force in the universe, you need to make good on the creation or cancel it out cleanly. Otherwise you are bucking the greatest power there is.

Here are the bare essentials of the art, learned by many difficult trials and errors.

Think carefully before you make an agreement. It is much easier to not make an agreement than it is to get out of one you no longer want to keep. Just ask a good matrimonial attorney if you have any doubts about this point.

Make only agreements that you feel a heart connection with. If you don't have heart behind the agreement, whether it's your child's baseball game or attending the annual shareholders' meeting, why bother? Agreements that are unimportant to you, but that you make anyway, have a tendency to come back and haunt you later because some intuitive person will perceive that you are not really there.

Scrupulously keep the agreements you make.

If you have a life any more complicated than, say, a sheepherder's, be sure to write agreements down. Taking them out of your mind and putting them on paper frees up more of your creative energy. A frequent component of business squabbles is the sentence "I wasn't sure we agreed to that...." These can be entirely avoided.

Honesty isn't the best policy. It's the only policy.

—HARLAN RANDOLPH

HOW TO CHANGE AN AGREEMENT THAT ISN'T WORKING

There's only one way. Communicate about it. Take a deep breath and tell the truth. The other person may or may not go along with the change. There may be an emotional explosion. You may not get what you want. But you'll never know until you talk about it.

The more you can tell the absolute truth about the situation, the better it will work. For example, if your big meeting with the boss coincides with your child's baseball play-off, tell the details about the conflict to the relevant person. How do you feel about it? Are you afraid, or confused? Give the raw data, the unresolved stuff inside you. People appreciate hearing it. It gives them the "real you" instead of the packaged version, and often allows a creative solution to emerge.

INTEGRITY IS A MATTER OF PHYSICS AS MUCH AS MORALITY

Although integrity sounds like a moral issue, it is even more fundamental. Integrity is a physics problem, and to fiddle with the laws of physics is to invite rapid disaster.

If you get out of step by not making good on your agreement, a domino effect is set in motion. Catch it quickly enough and you're usually fine. Ignore it or try to cover your tracks and watch what happens. The universe will not be messed with. Many people think of this as a moral issue, but long before there were morals—a human construction—there were the fundamental laws by which the universe was running itself. No doubt these laws will be operative long after the human experiment has run its course.

> *In the battle between you and the world,*
> *back the world.*
>
> —FRANK ZAPPA

There is a cosmic and yet highly practical reason all the mystics we interviewed for this book showed up on time for their interviews, no matter if they were coming from across town or across the country. They know that to make agreements is a sacred covenant between them and the universe. They know better than to mess with the forces of creation. They also know that to keep agreements is a statement of how much they value themselves and the essence of the person on the other end of the agreement.

STANDING ON ONE LEG: HOW NON-MYSTICS HANDLE AN INTEGRITY PROBLEM

When confronted with an integrity breach, non-mystics typically do one or more of several things:

Make Excuses: Like the fancy footwork of the matador, an excuse is an attempt to sidestep the consequences of having tempted fate. But most businesspeople people are smarter than bulls; they don't fall for the fancy footwork.

Pretend It Never Happened: Some ignore the integrity breach and proceed blithely as if things are all right, thus postponing the inevitable. Next time the message comes in, it comes in louder.

Execute the Messenger: Mystics thank the people who bring up the integrity breach. The ordinary person shuns them. In the Nixon inner circle all the truth tellers quit, got demoted or were fired, until all that remained were the liars. And we all know how that ended.

Get Defensive: Some people, particularly those of low self-esteem, stonewall or bite back because they misperceive the message as an attack. Their self-worth is fragile at best, so they think that being reminded of a broken agreement is a barb directed at their personhood rather than a wake-up call.

Send Up a Smokescreen: Caught in an integrity breach, some people fire off a barrage of complaints they've been nursing inside. They don't like the way the message was delivered or they've been mad about something else that they used as their excuse to break the agreement. Sometimes they are successful at getting people to fall for this shift of focus.

Compound the Felony: Others compound the felony by saying "The check's in the mail" when it still hasn't made it off their desk. Caught in one integrity breach, a step out of synchrony with the universe, they take a further step away from integrity, standing alone on one leg out where the high winds blow. Look out.

These moves are all the stuff of soap opera, but they happen all too frequently in the corporate realm. To walk the mystic path, study them carefully, and do the exact opposite: Thank the messenger, get the message, take action.

> *There's a difference between knowing the path and walking the path.*
>
> —TONY HSIEH,
> CEO, ZAPPOS

HOW MYSTICS HANDLE AN INTEGRITY PROBLEM

The surest mark of mystics at work is how they handle integrity lapses. Remember, mystics are not immune to integrity breaches, but they are quicker to fix them than the average person.

Part of the mind-set of the mystic is to greet feedback gracefully. Mystics take care to appreciate both the message and the messenger. They thank and often reward the person who says "You've broken an agreement" or "This isn't fair." Most people do not get this kind of direct feedback because the messenger is afraid to give it. Mystics typically place a higher value on truth than they do on their own comfort.

They are quick to acknowledge lapses they have perpetrated. They can say things like "I realize that I broke our agreement" and "I was not telling you the truth when I said...." Although they may make far fewer mistakes than the average person, they are quick to say "I made a mistake here" or "Looks like I was dead wrong on that issue." People with low self-esteem cannot admit mistakes or cop to a broken agreement: Being right is all they've got. Corporate Mystics will tell you they made a mistake as quickly as they'll tell you the time of day.

Mystics do not waste time with regret; they put their energy into solutions. Sometimes it's as simple as telling whatever truth wasn't told the first time around. Other times you must handle the wounded feelings of the person on the other end of the perpetration. An agreement may need to be renegotiated or an apology issued. Whatever the action, you won't know until you raise the question: "What needs to be done here to fix this and move on?"

Once you have determined that a painful phone call has to be made, it is wise to do it before you do anything else. Integrity problems fester faster once you know about them but before you've acted on them. Usually, what is required is a communication or an action, and sometimes both. If your employee has been stealing from Widow Smith's account, you have to replace the money, fire the employee, and give the widow a full accounting of the story. Act quickly and leave no loose ends.

The mystic's response can be broken into four steps.

First: Face squarely what happened.

The number one cause of integrity disasters is looking the other way, not facing them straight on in the early stages. Some of us postpone it for a lifetime. An example: A man who headed one of America's largest companies was having an affair with a charismatic woman, a vice-president some years his junior. As the buzz began to spread through the organization, his top aide told him that he needed to face the situation squarely. The aide later said that his boss literally looked out the window and changed the subject! The cost of not facing it squarely escalated quickly. Soon, with the board of directors on his back, the boss issued a heated denial, saying that he and the vice-president were "just friends." Nobody believed it, and time showed why. Later, after the ax had fallen, the two were quietly married.

The question remains: Why not just face things squarely and cop to them? The answer is the fear that most of us carry with us from junior high school on: We don't want to get caught and look stupid. Mystics know a secret that cures them of this fear: By the time we start getting scared of being caught and looking stupid, we've already been caught and we already look stupid. We have caught ourselves. Might as well admit it cheerfully and get on with it.

Second: Accept the situation.

Suppose you have cheated on your taxes. The first step—facing squarely what happened—means that you drop all the denial, excuse making, rationalizing, and avoidance. You admit it: You cheated.

Accepting goes deeper. It allows you to have a deep-body experience of reality. You haven't accepted something until you feel a shift deep in yourself. This may take time. It means giving up your final resistance to the truth. You accept the part of you that is a cheater. You acknowledge your greed, your irresponsibility, and whatever else motivates your cheating. You accept your cheating history, assuming it's happened before, and you open up to learning everything you need to know about the role cheating plays in your life. Accepting is a very comprehensive action. It may take months, not minutes. However, the moment you truly accept something, no matter how long it takes, you create an open space from which to create a new way of being.

Most of us are kept from genuine acceptance by two barriers. First, we often do not want to accept unpleasant or unsavory aspects of ourselves. But until we have faced and accepted these aspects—"I'm an alcoholic" or "I cheated"—

there is no clear space from which to generate change. Second, many people think that if they accept something they will be stuck with it forever. There is a rich paradox here. Not accepting something as it is keeps it in place. Accepting it begins the change process. We have it upside down. We need to understand that a full, deep-body acceptance of reality, exactly as it is, provides the springboard for change.

Third: Make a choice.

Now you must choose. Choosing has enormous power, especially if it comes from a clear space of acceptance. Failure to choose a new path of action causes as many integrity breaches as not facing or not accepting. The ordinary person thinks that not choosing keeps lots of options open. The mystic knows that not choosing keeps us mired in confusion and energy-draining drama. Perry Barlow faced a difficult choice when he took over as CEO of an Australian land-development firm. The preceding six months had been tied up in a dispute of whether to proceed with a resort-development project that violated an Aboriginal sacred site. The previous CEO's reputation had been eroded in the struggle, and Perry had been called in to bail out the company. He called a news conference his first day on the job and announced that the project would be scrapped. He became a hero overnight to the environmentalists, one of whom steered him to a piece of land that was beautifully suited to the project.

Fourth: Take action.

The fourth step sets you free. It asks you to focus on action: What do you need to do right now to set the situation right? Suppose you have faced and accepted that you cheated on your income tax. You have taken the third step, choosing to pay the money you owe. What is your fourth step? Is it to write the check and mail it? Is it to write the IRS and tell them what you've decided? You don't get back into integrity until you complete the necessary action step.

HIGH-FIRING
AS A STEP TO INTEGRITY

As you increase your ability to tell the truth and keep your agreements, you will find yourself held back by people who are not willing to play at a high level of integrity. You need to consciously free yourself from these entanglements. Whether or not you are in a position to actually terminate their employment, you can benefit from "high-firing" these people from your business and personal life.

High-firing takes guts, but it pays off very quickly. The rules for high-firing are simple: If you tell the truth reliably, you stop spending time with people who don't. If you keep your agreements, you avoid people who don't. You "fire" people who aren't functioning at your level, and by so doing you establish a free zone into which you can invite people who are.

High-firing requires you to look at your end of the relationship. You must be honest with yourself about the reasons you enrolled this person in your life. For many of us, the brutal truth is that carrying low-energy associates is a way of holding ourselves back. As long as we're saddled with energy-draining people, we have a good excuse for not being as successful as we might be.

Most firing done by non-mystics is not high-firing. One person simply gets mad at another, usually for some totally unconscious reason, and there is a noisy breakup. There is no intention to create integrity for each person. In high-firing, you work out your intentions first, before you sever your connection with the person. If you are kindhearted, you will probably want to give a warning. You sit down with the person and say, "I'm taking a major stand for truth and keeping agreements in my life. We haven't had a relationship in which we've had high integrity. Would you be willing to base our relationship on integrity from here on out?" Watch carefully the other person's reaction. If they get defensive or negative in any way, this predicts that they are not capable. You can give them a chance, if you want, but you may be disappointed. Most people, in retrospect, wish they had fired the person earlier and cleaner.

A fellow consultant shared this high-firing story with us: "When you challenged me to look at who was draining energy around me, I was resistant to it. As I checked out why I was defensive I uncovered a loyalty issue stemming from protecting my mother from my father. Dad was frequently abusive, and I took my mother's side in protecting her. But siding with her meant overlooking some of her bad habits, especially her hypercriticalness toward me and my sister. It was a lose-lose situation for me, putting myself in the middle. I realized I was doing the same thing in my organization. There was one contract employee who was a real energy drain. He produced a lot of revenue for me indirectly, but he also had a lot of bad habits I wasn't confronting. He was cheating on his wife in a particularly flagrant manner which had involved some unpleasant calls to me from two women in his life. I realized that failing to deal squarely with this situation was a replay of the pattern with my mother and father.

"I called a meeting with him and said we weren't going to work with him anymore. He became angry and abusive, using language that was eerily similar to my father's. I stayed pretty cool throughout, though, and at the end I walked out feeling light and free.

"The real magic happened just after the high-firing. I had been trying for a year to get on a national talk show to call attention to my book. Even though the book had been out for a year, suddenly two national shows booked me within three days. Although there's no way to prove it, my gut tells me that firing him made the space for this burst of good luck."

THE ULTIMATE PAYOFF

When you are in integrity, you are in step with the universe. If you say you will be at the corner of Vine and Ninth at twelve noon, you step into the creator role in the universe. You designate a future that does not yet exist and create an image of yourself there. If you actually show up on that corner at twelve noon, you are in a perfect time-space relationship with the universe. If you don't, you are out of step with time and space. So, the ultimate payoff for integrity is mastery of time and space. After acting with integrity for a while, you always seem to be in the right place at the right time. The universe seems to bend to your wishes.

The following true story will illustrate how the high-integrity person can move unimpeded through a universe fraught with danger, difficulty, and uncertainty. This example comes from corporate consultant Susan Snowe. Susan was leading a workshop on integrity in southern California. One of the agreements for the seminar was radical and stringent: If, at any time during the week, you were late for a session, you were out of the program. Period. No matter what the reason or the excuse. Since it was a very expensive training program, the motivation for integrity was high.

Susan tells the story: "Upon returning from a dinner break one evening a woman stood up and related the following experience. She had taken care of an errand during the break and was running tight on time. As she hurried out of a market with a bag of food, a man with a knife accosted her and demanded her money. Without thinking about it, she looked him in the eye and blurted out, 'I don't have time for this now. I have an agreement I can't break. I've got to go.' She ran to her car and sped away, leaving an astonished robber in the parking lot, staring at the departing car.

"She got to the seminar on time for the evening session, unrobbed and in integrity."

2

VISION:

LEADERSHIP BY INSPIRING CLEAR INTENTION

The key is to listen to your heart and let it carry you in the direction of your dreams. I've learned that it's possible to set your sights high and achieve your dreams and do it with integrity, character, and love. Each day that you're moving toward your dreams without compromising who you are you're winning

—Michael Dell,
CEO and Chairman, Dell Technologies

Integrity must precede vision. History has shown us the awesome cost of vision without integrity. A charismatic leader such as Hitler gets his people excited about a vision but leads them to doom because the vision is unsupported by integrity, rotten at the core. If your vision does not have a strong integrity base, expect disaster down the line. Begin by focusing on integrity, and your visions have a great deal of positive power in the world.

Integrity has a beneficial effect on the ability to see the future. It produces alignment in yourself, and just as in a well-aligned car, steering becomes easier.

If your integrity is unshakable, you have a clear grasp of present reality—and this helps you see where things are going. Particularly, you can see if the direction you're heading is causing the spirits of the people involved, you included, to contract, wither, or shrivel. There is no more powerful early warning that you are heading in the wrong direction. If you aspire to be a Corporate Mystic, combine your mastery of integrity with a careful study of visioning skills.

If we don't change the direction we're going,
we're likely to end up where we're headed.

—ANCIENT CHINESE PROVERB

Most business failures are failures of vision. By contrast, a clear vision often is the first step on the road to success. Many of the successful people we have encountered began their journey to success with an act of vision. Sometimes it was a simple act, like asking themselves that radical question, "What do I really want?" For others it was a more formal procedure of mocking up a desired future in their imagination.

Visionaries often have difficulties in corporations unless they are at the very top (and sometimes even then). Some of the most visionary people we encountered were often frustrated because they had to deal with two or three layers of noncreative, nonvisionary managers. Managers often do a thorough job of squelching ideas, but not such a good job of nurturing creative input from visionaries. Visionaries must bear some of the responsibility here, too. We have met many visionaries who were too thin-skinned to keep their visions flourishing when they encountered resistance.

There are several good reasons to develop visioning skills. Without vision, you have no proactive direction in which to organize the resources at your command. Vision allows you to create reality, not merely to react to it. Another major advantage of conscious visioning is how setbacks are perceived. If you have a clear vision of your goals and purposes, you will experience the inevitable setbacks as barriers on the path to something grand. If your vision is big enough, you'll view barriers as challenges rather than obstacles, to be studied with care as you navigate. Some people fall apart when setbacks are encountered. That's because their vision is not grand enough.

Every Corporate Mystic we interviewed for this book was a skilled visionary. Although the mental techniques they used were very different, they all knew how to transplant themselves into the future and describe the steps necessary to get there. Some of our mystics had these skills from early in their lives, while others had consciously worked to develop them. Corporate Mystics are also masters of something broader we will call intention. We will begin there.

WHAT IS INTENTION?

*Envision, create and believe in your own universe,
and the universe will form around you.*

—TONY HSIEH,
CEO ZAPPOS

Intention is a powerful force. Coming from a Latin word that means "to stretch toward," intention is the initial bending of your mind toward a target. It is the force that permeates the journey and the goal. A story from the medieval Christian tradition illustrates intention: A traveler came to a worksite and saw two men carrying stones. One man was working listlessly, with a sullen expression on his face, while the other man was cheerfully singing as he busily carried stone after stone. "What are you doing?" asked the traveler of the sullen worker. "Laying stone" was his reply. "What are you doing?" the industrious worker was asked. "Building a cathedral" was his reply. This is intention at work.

Intention precedes and inspires vision. Intention lives in the zone between potential and action, organizing the diffuse energy of potential and bringing it toward reality. Intention is also the ability to hold a visionary context in which all of your specific visions are organized. Inspired leadership is the ability to work from the zone of intention, so that your very being brings forth visionary thinking in your colleagues. This is important because great leaders do not want to have followers, they want to spawn more leaders. The old formulas such as "Management thinks up the job and workers carry it out" are clearly out of date. Ideally, everyone should have the ability to add his or her own unique visionary capabilities to the job at hand. But many of us, even the best and brightest, are handicapped by a lack of training in the skills of intention and visioning. You will need to bootstrap yourself and your colleagues up to a functional level of skill.

Think of intention as your overall way of getting to a place, not your map of the details. It is a vast goal that is at once measurable yet so large that it inspires people to become themselves visionaries within it. An intention is how you want the game to come out, both in content and process. It sets magic in motion. If you will make the decision, the saying goes, your subconscious will make the provision.

Teams at Komatsu, the Japanese maker of earth-moving equipment, spent a great deal of corporate think-time working to express their intention succinctly. Finally, they got it down to two words: "Encircle Caterpillar!" This intention says how they would like the whole enterprise to come out. It also expresses the sense of competition they will use to get there. With two words they formed an intention that also worked well as a rallying cry. Your intention can and should be expressed this concisely. Another good model, developed by a team at Coca-Cola: "A Coke within arm's reach of everyone in the world." Whether or not you like Coke, you experience movement in your mind and body when you hear that intention.

If your intention is clear, you create an electric field of possibility that actually pulls creativity out of yourself and those around you. This is the real power of intention. It inspires you in ways you could not predict. When Komatsu developed their intention—Encircle Caterpillar!—they did not know exactly how they were going to do it. Far from it, in fact. One of the hallmarks of a good intention is that it should be bigger than your current abilities. As their clarity with this intention grew, they found themselves devising technology and marketing strategies commensurate with the size of their intention.

If you know exactly how to get to your goal, you need a bigger intention. Growth and excitement in individuals and companies come from stretching to achieve things that may not have seemed possible even a week earlier.

The secret of life is to have a task,
something you devote your entire life to...
and the most important thing is—
it must be something you cannot possibly do!

—Henry Moore

What we need is more people who
specialize in the impossible.

—Theodore Roethke

HOW TO CREATE A POWERFUL INTENTION

Kate was once in charge of a large project that brought together executives of six major semiconductor suppliers and their eight largest distributors to pool some of their data for the common good. Kate: "I was very excited because of the groundbreaking nature of this cooperative project. After we were under way I got a call one day saying that the largest distributor was backing out. I was deeply disappointed. Although the project would still be useful, having the largest player pull out would weaken the paradigm-shifting collaborative effort. My heart actually ached because I so much wanted them to pull together.

"We went ahead, though, and I set the intention in my heart of having the project yield the breakthrough we were looking for regardless of who played and who didn't. I held the intention that it be a win for the players and even for the company that had dropped out. I resolved to share the findings with them, even though they weren't sharing with the others. After a few months we had processed most of the data, but we uncovered a software problem that we couldn't figure out how to correct. As we were puzzling over it I got a call from the head of the company which had backed out: They had decided to play! Everybody was elated, and even agreed to wait six weeks for the new data to be integrated so that we could present a unified set of findings. During the six weeks we got our software problem fixed, so the delay turned out to be a blessing for all concerned."

BEWARE OF COVERT INTENTIONS

Most of us have values that are sacred to us, values like passionate commitment, complete integrity, and warm regard for others. Yet we do not always act in accordance with these high intentions. The road to hell, the old saying goes, is paved with good intentions. Why is that?

It is because we have covert intentions, hidden from the light, that trip us up when we move in our chosen directions. The only way to clear ourselves of these covert intentions is to bring them out into the light and openly acknowledge that we carry them.

A Corporate Mystic we interviewed shared this story: "Throughout the development of [a new technological device] I missed one deadline after another. The CEO kept calling me on the carpet and I kept saying, 'This isn't like me' and 'I've never missed deadlines before.' Finally one evening after one of our consulting sessions, I let go of being defensive and acknowledged the negative intention. I said, 'Okay, I'm committed to missing deadlines. That's what the results say. I have an intention to miss deadlines.' Now why would I have that intention? About two seconds after I asked myself that question the lightbulb came on in my head. This was the biggest project of my career, and I wanted desperately to succeed in the eyes of the CEO, who was a father figure to me. But at the same time I was putting the face of my father's criticalness on him, too. It was as if I was trying to set it up so I failed in his eyes. I realized I was carrying a conscious intention to succeed and an unconscious intention to fail. Because I had failed so often in the eyes of my father, I had embodied an intention to fail that was getting in my way."

One of our clients was a peace activist of national reputation who had founded a political organization. His conscious intention was nonviolence and world harmony, yet his organization was in trouble because of his violent explosions of anger. His wife had also left him because he hit her on several occasions. It was obvious from his actions that he carried a covert intention to harm others that was sabotaging his stated intention to promote peace.

He was very comfortable expressing his intention to promote world harmony—he could make that speech at the drop of a hat—yet he became angry at us when we asked him to acknowledge his intention toward violence. He could easily say, "I'm committed to world peace," but he had trouble admitting, "I'm committed to getting my own way even through violence." Yet this intention was the one that was ruining his life.

There is only one way to find out what your unconscious intentions are: Look at any negative results you produce. Every Corporate Mystic needs to know this principle in his or her bones. In the case of our peace activist client, the results said, "I'm committed to expressing violence." After several sweaty days of consultation, he was courageous enough to acknowledge both his violent and his peaceful aspects. He confronted the roots of his violence in his tortured relationship with an alcoholic and abusive father. He also discovered that he had become a peace activist partly in reaction to his father, an "I'll show you!" intention.

Only when he acknowledged all this did the violent outbursts cease. His organizational and marital problems smoothed out once he cleared his covert intentions.

> *The first peace, which is the most important,*
> *is that which comes within the souls of people when*
> *they realize their relationship, their oneness,*
> *with the universe and all its powers,*
> *and when they realize at the center of the universe*
> *dwells the Great Spirit,*
> *and that this center is really everywhere.*
> *It is within each of us.*
>
> —BLACK ELK

THE INTENTION OF WHOLENESS

If you would operate in the mystic realm, you must operate from a clear intention of wholeness and connection. In words, the intention might be expressed like this: "I consciously intend to have [this project or enterprise] benefit the wholeness of ourselves and the environment around us." If you build in a metavision of wholeness at the beginning, projects will work more smoothly. If you pretend you are not connected to the whole, that doesn't stop you from being connected. It just stops you from feeling connected. Mystics have a nearly reflexive ability to ask questions like: How am I not participating in the whole? Who else is not operating from an appreciation of the whole? Where is connection being broken or impeded?

A former high-tech global president shared this story: "Before I moved to my international role and started interfacing with so many other cultures, I was reasonably myopic. Until I sat in forests with trees that were four thousand years old, I didn't understand how long life really was and how fragile it was, how important it was to get our lives to fall in harmony with nature." This is an awareness of wholeness, and one can see how powerfully it might shape the future visioning of this executive as he works on new projects.

THE INTENTION OF BALANCE

Balance is the Corporate Mystic's second key intention. As we proceed toward our chosen visions, we need to keep ourselves and our enterprises in a state of balance. The notion of balance pervades the mystic worldview. For Taoists, yin and yang are in eternal balance throughout nature itself, and it is our task as humans to harmonize ourselves with this balance. A pinnacle concept of Navajo metaphysics, *hozho*, says that we must walk in harmony with ourselves and the earth, lest we do damage to both.

Businesspeople go out of balance in several common areas.

Logic and emotion. Nature has given us logic, which resides in the neocortex, and it has also given us emotion, which lives beneath the cortex in the limbic system. Logic is indispensable for success in business, but businesspeople get in trouble when they leave behind their feelings. Feelings were here long before logic evolved, so extra attention must be given to staying in communication with them. Emotions like fear, anger, and sadness flicker across the screen of our consciousness all day long. You don't have to report each one of them to the world, but you do know what you're feeling when you're feeling it.

Home and work. No matter what rung of the corporate ladder you're on, constant vigilance is required lest the demands of the workplace eat up your home life. The higher you climb, the more imperative it becomes to walk in and out of your front door each day with a clear mind and an open heart. In our consulting work, we find that imbalance between home and work is often the most common subject of conversation among executives. Single or married, living in a mansion or a studio apartment, we all need a life outside work. It is easy to get out of balance, given the demands of the contemporary corporate environment.

Striving versus enjoying. The tightened jaw and the furrowed brow are signs not of zeal but of imbalance. Are you so focused on outcome that you are not enjoying the process? If so, find out how you can lighten up and have a better time. You might even discover, as many have, that they get more done when they ease up a little. As consultants, one of the quickest ways we diagnose the health of an organization is by the amount of fun people appear to be having. They are getting the job done, and they are having a good time doing it. There is a feeling we call the "fun-buzz" that successful organizations have. The fun-buzz is made up of relaxed busyness, pleasant interactions, laughter, and engagement. One of the most exciting things as organizational consultants is watching the fun-buzz begin and build as the health of the organization improves.

The intention of balance changed the life of John Fine, a real estate developer and entrepreneur based in California and Colorado. "During the first ten years of my working life I was so focused on my projects that I hardly stopped to take a breath. Even when I was hiking in the mountains I was planning projects in my mind. Then I had two wake-up calls in the same week. While jogging (and of course discussing a real estate project with the guy I was running with) I developed chest pains. I went to the doctor in a panic, but it turned out to not be a heart problem but an emotional one. My wife had been telling me for a year that I needed to open up to my emotions more, so I could find out why I got into such rages when things didn't go my way. When I came home from the doctor and told her my heart was okay, she said it was not okay at all. In her opinion I was hiding so much anger and sadness that it didn't matter how many shopping malls I built. I was never going to be happy unless I took a look inside. Further, she said she had been thinking about leaving the relationship because I was never really there. She said, 'I didn't marry you just to show up at public events with you. I want a real marriage.' I was stunned, and I sat down on the floor in the living room to mull it over. About ten seconds after I sat down, I burst into tears. I don't think I'd cried since I was a kid. I couldn't have stopped crying even if I'd wanted to. I found myself babbling to my wife about how cheated I felt about not having a childhood. My father had a heart attack when I was eleven, and I took over his role in the family. I had as many wrinkles in my brow at fourteen as I had now at forty-four.

"Thank goodness Annie didn't try to stop me from crying or tell me it was all going to be better. When I got through, which was maybe twenty minutes later, I got up and wrote some new 'vows,' as I thought of them. I vowed to play as much as I worked, love as much as I worked, smile as much as I scowled. I actually put these on the wall in my office and my den. I asked Annie for six months to make good on these vows. If I wasn't making progress on them that she could see, we would amicably divorce. One of the proudest days of my life was when that six months was up. I said, 'Well?' She hugged me and said that I had changed my life. That was twenty years ago, and we're still together."

One direct outcome of this personal transformation was that John instituted an intention of balance in his organization. Friday mornings started with "balance" meetings, to which he invited guest speakers from different backgrounds to address the issue of wholeness and balance. The working retreats held once a year took on this theme, also. Significant others were invited for the first time, and off-site locations were chosen with the idea of balance in mind.

*Working harder is not a sustainable solution,
and it's not how people meet their destiny.
It's time to get more creative.
Instead of choosing one thing we love
over something else we love, we must ask,
"How can I do both?"
And then we can find solutions.*

—Maynard Webb,
Founder, Webb Investment Network
and former COO of eBay

THE INTENTION OF GRATITUDE

Your visions will become real more smoothly if they emerge from a context of gratitude. Many people have gratitude backwards: They are willing to express it only after something good happens to them. Corporate Mystics know a secret: Express gratitude first—lead with gratitude—and you will get gratitude back in double measure. Each new step toward the future is taken in gratitude for the way things are now. And what if the way things are now is not to your liking? All the more reason to appreciate them, for the beginnings of change live in a deep acceptance of the present reality. The Corporate Mystic thinks: Things are the way they are; now let's go about changing them. The ordinary person thinks: Things can't possibly be the way they are! or Whose fault is it that things are the way they are? Denial and blame have no place in the mystic tool bag. A clear-eyed look at the present and a vision of the future: These are the tools the mystic uses to steer through an ever-changing universe.

A good question to ask is: What could I do in my life and in my organization to foster a pervasive tone of gratitude? If you were going to honor each person you work closely with in a singular way that moved them, how would you do it? For example, in one of the authors' organizations, we put considerable attention into gratitude. Gay: "We have a diverse group of people who work with us, so our challenge is to express our gratitude for them in ways that are particularly suited to them. One of our people loves travel. At the end of one very good year, we gave her a bonus of a trip to Hawaii. Another person has a high value on education. In her case, we help her financially with her schooling, and we also make time available to her for it. We come up with ideas based on the question, 'What could we best do to express our gratitude?' and then we consult with them about the details."

Begin with a moment of reflection: Who in your life are you most grateful for? How could you best show your gratitude for the people around you? Take a few seconds right now to feel appreciation for them.

The miracle is this—
the more we share,
the more we have.

—Leonard Nimoy,
Actor, Spock in Star Trek

THE TYRANNY OF IS

Some visionaries may be born free from the tyranny of "is." But the rest of us have to break free of it. What is this tyranny? It is a view of the world that keeps you trapped in a limited set of options. Here's how it works. Many people act from a vision-killing superstition: that their interpretation of reality is the same as reality itself. When the steam locomotive was new, a breakthrough in technology made it possible for it to exceed thirty miles an hour. With the speed of forty miles an hour in sight, a debate broke out, even in the medical literature of the time. One learned doctor said that it was common knowledge that the human body would explode at forty miles an hour. That's the way it "is," he said.

Usually the tyranny has its stranglehold on companies when everyone agrees on the interpretation of current conditions.

"This company is in decline."
"We are in a recession."

"The president is an ineffective leader."
"This problem is unsolvable."

When we are in the grip of the tyranny of "is," there is no possibility for change. We see the condition, whatever it may be, as intractable.

> *Notice the difference between what happens when a man says to himself "I have failed three times," and what happens when he says "I am a failure."*
>
> —S. I. HAYAKAWA

Visionary leaders break free of the tyranny, and they get others to break free. They look carefully at all the places they are operating out of "is." They step back, separate out their interpretation from reality, and find out what needs to be done.

Begin by changing your verbs. Avoid "is" and "are." Instead of "The president is an ineffective leader," try "I disagree with the president's choice to..." or "The president didn't produce a successful labor negotiation when he said he would." When you take the "is" out, you open up the possibility for change to occur. "Is" and "are," since they are statements of being, do not point to actions that can be taken. When you unfreeze your perceptions from "is" and "are," you move toward action: What can the president do to move the labor negotiations along? What can you do to help?

THE TYRANNY OF BECAUSE

There is another tyrant you must battle in your company and in yourself. It is the tyranny of "because."

"I was late because my alarm clock didn't go off."
"Profits are declining because of the recession."
"I am getting divorced because my spouse is too critical."

"Women make poor leaders because they are too emotional."
"You can't be honest with people because it will damage the relationship."

When you say "because," you claim that you know the reason something happened. You justify your course of action because of an extraneous factor. And you know what? Sometimes you're right. However, more often than not the reason you claim is not the sole reason or even the most important reason for something. If you think you are late because your alarm didn't go off, you are overlooking other interesting possibilities. You might be late because you have a self-sabotage program operating. Or because you don't really want to be doing what you're doing. Once you lock in on a certain "because," you don't go any further. When you say "because," you stop the inquiry process.

"Because" is a vision killer. One of the most common phrases heard in early visioning sessions with companies is "We can't do that because..." There can be a dozen reasons: not enough money, not enough resources, not enough time. Another common one these days: "My plan was side-tracked because I wasn't willing to play politics." "Becauses" are dangerous because they keep us from looking inside ourselves. A "because" stops the inquiry process, which must be ongoing for individuals and companies to succeed.

Here is how a Corporate Mystic handled a potentially troublesome "because." As a newly appointed vice-president, she had difficulty getting people on the executive team to listen to her ideas. As she tells it: "At first I blamed it on the usual reasons, like 'They don't listen to me because I'm a woman.' But as long as I held that point of view, nothing changed. So I shifted my strategy. In the meetings I observed the vice-president who had the most power. I respected him enormously, plus he had the ear of the president. When I simply observed him instead of envying him, I learned several crucial things. First, he presented his ideas in a bottom-line format; he gave supporting details only when he was asked. He didn't present a flurry of data, as I had been doing. Second, when he encountered resistance he didn't argue with the other people. Rather, he asked them a lot of questions! In other words, he was genuinely interested in understanding their concerns. What often happened was that people would talk themselves out of their concerns as he listened carefully to their points of view. Looking back, I can see that my career took a major upturn when I quit indulging in 'becauses' and started looking for people I could really learn from instead of envy."

Visionary leaders put all "becauses" under the microscope, especially the ones everybody agrees on. Often the biggest breakthroughs come from finding the "because" that underlies the most intractable conditions.

> *If you've always done it that way,*
> *it's probably wrong.*
>
> —CHARLES KETTERING

THE ZONE OF COMPLACENCY

Corporate Mystics learn to work outside the zone of complacency. Non-mystics live in the zone, and usually die there. Your zone of complacency is that complicated batch of thoughts, feelings, beliefs, and convictions designed to keep you from becoming uncomfortable. Most of us have one, whether we are flush with success or broken and battered. It is worth our careful attention because it has slain more good visions than a million critics.

Many people think that their discomfort is all the reason they need not to do something. Corporate Mystics look at discomfort completely differently: It is something to be met squarely on the way to wherever they've chosen to go. One of our corporate clients calls now and then to get a phone consultation on some project she is working on. Often she begins by saying, "I've hit a couple of speed bumps here lately, and I want to find out what I can do to smooth things out." She views obstacles as speed bumps—just a minor feature of the road—and by slowing down a little and being careful, she can get back up to speed.

The zone of complacency develops a life of its own inside us. When it is challenged, it throws several types of feelings at us. These feelings are smoke screens, designed to discourage us from going outside the zone.

The first smoke screen is fear. Wired into our bodies hundreds of thousands of years ago, fear programs us to run, fight, faint, or freeze. That is just what the zone of complacency would have you do. You come up with an outrageous vision of yourself—"I'd like to start my own business instead of working for Fred"—and the zone kicks in with fear. It wants you to run from this vision or better yet, freeze where you are. Our zone of complacency thinks that safety comes from running or freezing. Once we're in fear, the whole world looks different.

> *The very thing you fear could be the best thing to ever happen to you.*
>
> —MICHAEL DELL,
> CEO AND CHAIRMAN, DELL TECHNOLOGIES

> *When we're afraid, everything rustles.*
>
> —SOPHOCLES

When we dream of a bigger future for ourselves, we invoke its fears as well. We need to look unflinchingly at those fears if we are going to design a better future. Even a question that seems relatively straightforward—"How will Fred and I get financing?"—can have its roots in a much more fundamental fear: of aging, death, poverty, diminished capacity, criticism, loss of love, ill health. If we have not dealt with such fears, our ability to see the future is clouded. This act of averting our eyes, even slightly, will keep us from the level of comfort with the future that is required to make our home there.

The second smoke screen is guilt. You make a move that takes you out of the zone and you start to hear voices like:

"Who do you think you are?"

"If you're successful you'll outdo your dad."

"If you're successful nobody will like you. It's lonely at the top."

Guilt is really based on anger that was directed at you long ago for being gifted. It is the burden the gifted person drags into adult life. Long, long ago, someone—usually a parent or a sibling—drummed these negative messages into your mind. The drumming was so subtle and successful that you now think that these thoughts belong to you. They don't, except that you've internalized them and let them rattle around in your head. Now is the time to take a deep breath and let them go.

The third smoke screen is a lingering sense of our own unworthiness. If you have a shred of this left over from childhood—and most of us do—the zone of complacency will find it and use it to keep you locked in the zone. At least a dozen top-level Corporate Mystics have told us that they are flooded with a deep sense of their unworthiness just before they launch a big, new vision and just after they've tasted a big success. And you can see why: They are operating outside their zone of complacency.

Although it seems to work against us, let's not make the zone of complacency an enemy. Befriending the zone of complacency is the healing maneuver. To befriend the zone, let's first acknowledge that we are powerfully attracted to the comfortable and predictable. It's safe and secure, and wouldn't that be nice for a change? There is one part of us that is a comfort seeker, pure and simple. Accept and love that part of you, just as it is. But we also need to honor the risk taker within us. Most creative people have a strong drive that challenges the zone of complacency. It is the drive to explore the unknown, to bring into being something that never existed before, to soar into the high reaches where the air is thin but the big breezes blow.

The real trouble with the zone of complacency is that it expands very quickly. The zone gets bigger every time we make a decision to sacrifice an adventurous vision in favor of comfort. Unless we're very careful, pretty soon the zone of complacency has taken over our living space. We retreat to the zone a few times to avoid the risky business of life, and one day we wake up to find we can't get out of it.

But the zone can also shrink in the wink of an eye. All you need to do is make a few decisions outside the zone and—poof!—you're a player. No longer in thrall to the seductions of the zone, you are free to form visions that are uncontaminated by it.

WHAT DO I WANT?

Vision starts from the answer to a simple question: What do I really want? or What do I most want for this organization? One day the answer might be a new quality of personal interaction around the office. The next day you might get an entirely different answer, one that launches a new product line.

Corporate Mystics live in this question, asking it so frequently—even unconsciously—that their presence inspires others to start asking it.

> *The indispensable first step*
> *to getting the things you want out of life is this:*
> *Decide what you want.*
>
> —BEN STEIN

Questions of this nature—What do I most want for this company?—are powerfully transformative. When you ask them in a genuine state of inquiry you get brand-new information from your creative mind. But even when nothing comes, you are still doing something important. You are taking full responsibility for the creative direction of the company. You are becoming a source of creativity.

A mystic recalls a thrilling moment in the evolution of his business: "I had been on the bandwagon for creativity within the company for a long time, trying to get everybody inspired to think of creative ways to improve their particular area. One moment made it worthwhile. I was passing by the mailroom and stuck my head in to say hello. One of the staff, a minimum-wage part-timer, was writing a memo to her supervisor. In it she was proposing three changes in the mailroom operation. When I asked her where she'd gotten the ideas, she pointed to the question I'd asked everyone to post on the wall of their area: What do I most want for this company? She said she'd gone to bed the night before thinking about the question, and the three ideas had been floating through her mind when she woke up."

Kate organized a team-building retreat for a high-tech executive and the eight people who reported directly to him. One of the activities asked them each to draw a picture of themselves doing something that represented who they were at the core. Two of the managers were men in their fifties who hardly knew each other, yet they drew almost identical pictures. Both drew themselves working with older people in an eldercare facility. This represented the core heartfulness that was important for them to express. Of course, they and the whole team were dumbfounded that this shared vision had emerged; it did indeed bring the team closer together. More importantly, though, the bond between these two men increased with several rewarding outcomes. They began to meet midway between their two facilities, first to deepen their friendship and ultimately to find ways to express this passion in their current jobs. They also brainstormed a special project that would allow them to get more familiar with the actualities of eldercare.

Wherever you are in the corporate hierarchy, you are in a perfect position to look around and find out what you want, both for yourself and for the company. Often it only takes a few seconds to come up with an answer. Then, expand your horizons by asking other people: What do you most want? Many people have never been asked that question; to ask it could change someone's life for the better.

> *By believing passionately in something*
> *that still does not exist, we create it. The nonexistent*
> *is whatever we have not sufficiently desired.*
>
> —NIKOS KAZANTZAKIS

DEVELOPING NO-LIMITS VISION

What if there were no limits to what you could create? What if you could bring things into being through the powers you already possess? Well, this actually seems to be the way things work. Up until a hundred-and-some years ago there was no such thing as right and left shoes. If the shoe didn't fit you had to wear it anyway. There was even resistance to the idea at first. Why bother? Who cares? Shoes work okay the way they are! But somebody had a vision: Somebody hatched an idea in the mind, then transformed it into physical reality. Now just about ten billion feet walk around in an idea that nobody had even thought worth thinking before the last century.

Mystics know that they can't have everything they want: There is not enough time to manifest and enjoy everything you want. The mystic knows this and is careful to choose deeply desired heart-wants. Part of maturity, both in spirituality and in business, is to realize that you can't have everything, but that if you choose carefully you can have anything.

> *"One can't believe impossible things."*
> *"I daresay you haven't had much practice," said the Queen. "When I was your age, I always did it for half-an-hour a day. Why, sometimes I've believed as many as six impossible things before breakfast."*
>
> —LEWIS CARROLL

On a corporate level, this idea applies a thousandfold. As we travel on our consulting rounds, we find that the successful companies are doing a great deal of work on refining and narrowing their focus. They are selecting their customer demographics very carefully, and they are listening—really listening—to what those people want and need. The days of the corporate dinosaur are numbered; the large companies are often so unwieldy that they cannot respond to changes rapidly enough. The same problem faces individuals. If we have not narrowed our focus to choose carefully what we want, we cannot focus energy in the laser-like fashion that today's environment requires.

> *Listen, listen, listen.*
> *You can learn from anybody and everybody.*
>
> —ARNOLD DONALD,
> CEO, CARNIVAL CRUISES

The key is really two keys in one: choice and focus. You have the power of decision with regard to your wants. The word *decide* comes from the Latin and means "to cut off," as in cutting off your other alternatives. Once you've done that, your job becomes to focus on your chosen goal until you get the outcome you want.

STEP OUTSIDE THE BOX

Corporate Mystics take care to have visions that are grand enough to keep them inspired. Your goals should always be stretch goals, ones that you have no ready-made strategy for achieving. If you are always inside the box of known possibilities, you don't give your imagination the stretch it needs each day to keep it flourishing.

You must always do the thing you think you cannot do.

—ELEANOR ROOSEVELT

Mystics hone the ability to be in the present and in the future at the same time. Paradoxically, the skill of relaxing into the present opens up greater power to envision the future. Some people experience pain or despair when there is a gap between where they are and where they want to be. The mystic has learned to relax in the gap, to hold the goal lightly yet with unwavering intent. Corporate Mystics know a secret: Success is possible only when you are fully present—being there, wherever you are. They put their attention on their wandering attention, bringing it back to the present, here where I am. By doing this over and over again, they learn to relax into the gap. If your goals are big enough, there will always be a gap. Might as well enjoy it.

Take a step or two outside the box. What would be the most unreasonably positive future you could imagine for yourself? For your organization?

Think six impossible things before breakfast tomorrow.

I am looking for a lot of men who have an infinite capacity to not know what can't be done.

—HENRY FORD

DEALING WITH IDEA-SLAYERS

The truth is this: The better the idea, the more resistance it is likely to stir up. The best strategy is to expect resistance and try to bring it to the surface at the first presentation. While much of the resistance will be based on fear of change, some of it will contain valuable feedback. Visionaries who shrink from conflict often try to keep the resistance under the rug, only to find that it surfaces later covertly. If possible, confront every concern, ridicule, excuse, and fear up front. Provide counterarguments to these concerns, and expect that these counterarguments will flush up even more resistance. In a better world there would be fewer pigheaded people, but meanwhile visionaries need to cultivate their ability to handle resistance to new ideas. If you get stonewalled completely, thank your colleagues for their input and ask if they would be open to hearing a refined version at a later date. Usually they will say yes to help you save face; they will be shocked when you actually come back in a month or so with a revised plan.

It would be easier if the only resistance we met came from outside. The real problem, though, lies within. The source of much of the resistance that stops us comes from our own beliefs about our limitations.

Ignore the people who tell you it won't work and hire the people who embrace your vision.

—MICHAEL DELL,
CEO AND CHAIRMAN, DELL TECHNOLOGIES

We have met the enemy, and it is us.

—WALT KELLY

The stubborn obstacles we encounter outside ourselves are best regarded as signposts pointing to our own internalized resistance. The Corporate Mystic sees resistance as a friendly part of ourselves that is trying to point out risks and refine our communication skills. By honing our skills we can deal with the vast array of different people out in the world. If we see resistance as "out there," it locks us into an us versus them model that can be very destructive.

The real message here is that enlightened perseverance is necessary to bring about change in the corporate world. Visionaries must learn to expect resistance, both inside and outside themselves, and surf on the edge of it rather than letting it overwhelm them. Your own passion and dedication have to be bigger than other people's attachment to the way things have been, their fear of change and of losing control.

FUTURE-VISION

Corporate Mystics have an ability to stand in the future and take a look around, then to use the power of this imagined future to pull themselves and their organizations toward it. Most people, trapped unknowingly in their conditioning, sit in the past, which causes them to create a limited present and very little vision of the future. If you are sitting in the past, you may even resent the present and try to sabotage those who are committed to the future.

If you want to become a Corporate Mystic, stand in the future and look back toward the present. Get yourself thoroughly grounded in the future. Be there, and get comfortable seeing the world from that perspective. It is not important for you to have a detailed picture of the future, but it is crucial to plant one foot there so that the other foot will be motivated to follow.

Imagination is more important than knowledge.

—ALBERT EINSTEIN

John F. Kennedy enjoyed telling the story of small boys in Ireland who, when they came to a fence they were afraid to climb, would throw their hats over first so they would have to go after them. Throw your hat into the future, and you will be inspired to do whatever you can to follow it.

Another reason to become skilled in future-vision is so that you won't sabotage success when it begins to happen. If you step into the future and try it on, your body and mind have an opportunity to get comfortable with it. Once you've developed comfort with a positive future, you are less likely to trip yourself up when it unfolds. We are all conditioned to be afraid of the unknown, and even a positive unknown can rattle us. Future-vision allows you to establish yourself comfortably in an imagined positive future.

Now, in your imagination, locate yourself in the best future you can think of. Go out five years. What are you doing? What is your organization like? From the future, look back toward today. What did you do to get to that positive future?

> *What would you attempt to do if you knew*
> *you could not fail?*
>
> —Robert Schuller

3

INTUITION:

LEADERSHIP BY CALLING FORTH FULL POTENTIAL

> *People with high levels of personal mastery do not set out to integrate reason and intuition. Rather, they achieve it naturally—as a by-product of their commitment to use all the resources at their disposal. They cannot afford to choose between reason and intuition, or head and heart, any more than they would choose to walk on one leg or see with one eye.*
>
> —PETER SENGE

Some call it a "gut feeling," while others speak of an intuitive "flash." The dictionary says that *intuition* is "direct knowing of something without the conscious use of reasoning." It is what you might use to:

- Make a personnel decision.
- Tune in to where the problems are in a particular project.
- Get your timing right on an investment.
- Come up with a new market for an existing product.

Intuition is a natural gift, something to which we all have access. It is also a talent, something we can fine-tune with practice. The main reason intuition is so important is this: It is a clear sign that you are connecting with your inner spiritual guidance system. Intuition is a direct signal from your deepest self that you are navigating from your true center. When intuition is not working for you, it is a sign that you need to refresh your connection with your center. As an archbishop of Canterbury once said, "When I pray, miracles happen. When I don't, they don't." The same is true with intuition. When it's there, you can rest assured that you have been nurturing your connection with your own soul in some way. When it's not there, it's time to spend some time in meditation, or by a waterfall, or in your office with the door closed.

Intuition is a high-skill area of Corporate Mystics. As leaders, they must be in touch with the intuitive as well as the logical aspects of themselves. When the heart and soul connection is missing, no amount of data will fill the gap. As Father Theodore Hesburgh, former president of Notre Dame, once said of leaders, "You cannot blow an uncertain trumpet." The combination of intuition and logic gives the corporate leader a stance of unity from which to lead.

> *The leader who would create a vision sufficiently compelling to motivate associates to superior performances must draw on the intuitive mind.*
>
> —JOHN NAISBITT AND PATRICIA ABURDENE

Integrity and vision are precursors to the full use of your intuition. Intuition works better when you are in a state of integrity. When you are out of integrity, the noise from all your integrity incompletions tends to drown out the subtle signals from intuition.

Intuition also works better when you know where you're going. Vision is a great liberator of intuition. Creative detours appear most benignly in the journeys of people who are already on their way to somewhere important. As Louis Pasteur said, "Chance favors the prepared mind." Echoing this, one of our Corporate Mystics said: "Intuition favors the quiet, open mind." Integrity helps quiet the mind by eliminating the noise caused by lying and breaking agreements. Vision clears the mind by giving it a general focus and direction.

Intuition is not something you can learn from a book; you need to practice it experientially, experimentally, and frequently. Even our best information about intuition will not ultimately make you more intuitive. Spending time in the vast spaces of your own mind is what will do it. The last section of the book—"The Disciplined Mystic"—includes a very reliable method of opening to intuition that has been tested thousands of times. We encourage you to turn to this exercise after mastering the information in the present section, and give yourself plenty of practice time to get comfortable with it.

None of the ideas in this chapter is theoretical; all come from real people who use them in the heat of action. Keep in mind, though, that intuition is not an exact science for the best of its practitioners. Take what appeals to you, try it out experimentally, and feel free to modify and reject anything that doesn't work for you. At the very least you will experience the satisfaction of opening up an often mysterious realm for your own learning.

The intuitive mind will tell the thinking mind where to look next.

—Dr. Jonas Salk

INTUITION PLUS LOGIC: THE CORPORATE MYSTIC'S WINNING FORMULA

Chance does indeed favor the prepared mind, so we are not suggesting throwing out logic and doing everything by gut. But logic is only part of our mind's capabilities; since we've got intuition, why not learn to use it? The great value of intuition is that it helps us come up with solutions that cannot be seen by the clear light of logic. It is a way of tapping the vast riches of the unknown. If logic is the sun, intuition is the moon. Both can be appreciated by the thoughtful leader.

Many corporate leaders we know have a harmonious working relationship between intuition and logic. When we ask them how they got it, some of them say it's always been there. They say that their thinking strategies have not changed since childhood. Others tell us that they had to make a conscious commitment to using all of themselves. In many cases, the imbalance was originally in the direction of logic. They received feedback that they were too data-oriented and made a decision to open up to more of their intuitive capabilities. In a few cases, highly intuitive people had to balance themselves in favor of more logic and reasoning capabilities.

> *Intuition isn't some kind of magical clairvoyance that allows you to short-circuit informed decision making. It must first be fed with data, experience, and even the combined intuition of others before you can render an effective judgement.*
> *I also find that emotions of the day can have a dramatic impact on how your intuition interprets all these signals, so for the biggest of decisions I try to understand what else, often outside of work, might be creating a bias in my thinking. The old adage of 'sleeping on it' is often helpful in these situations.*
>
> —Brian Sharples,
> Founder, Former Chairman and CEO, HomeAway

YOUR CREATIVE THINK-TIME IS YOUR MOST IMPORTANT DAILY BUSINESS ACTIVITY

As one Corporate Mystic put it: "If I take twenty minutes a day of pure think-time, my day runs smoothly. If I get 'too busy' and forget to take my magic twenty minutes, things often feel slightly off all day. I've learned to notice when I'm drifting off course. Then it's time to go in my office, close the door, and look out the window for a little while."

Some of the mystics we interviewed for this book took ten minutes, others an hour. Some looked out the window, while others closed their eyes and hummed a mantra. But almost all of them had a way of building creative think-time into their day. They referred to their creative think-time in different words:

"Integration"
"Digesting data"
"Recharging my batteries"
"Accessing the creative zone"
"Resting and roaming"

But they were all talking about a similar process: going inside and drawing on their own inner resources. One manager put it bluntly: "Most businesspeople would not mess up half as much if they just took a few minutes to think. Just close the door and do nothing for a little while. A lot of the busywork that clutters up the business day is just a symptom of not enough think-time."

It takes discipline to make time in your day for creative thinking, and even fiercer discipline to protect this time from the ever-present demands on it. Those who do will reap rich rewards, both in increased productivity and a greater sense of working from one's true depth.

The really valuable thing is intuition.

—ALBERT EINSTEIN

GETTING A BETTER INTUITIVE HIT RATE

Your intuitions will improve to the extent that you can step outside your beliefs, opinions, and biases about the way things are. Think of biases as the noise that you hear instead of the clear signal of greater possibility. You might notice that your intuitions are very clear in one area of your life but very poor in another area. One mystic put it this way: "My hits were very accurate about work, but in the area of relationships I seemed to have little or no intuitive skill. As I studied this problem I came to see that I was carrying a lot more baggage with me about relationships than I was about work. At work I could look dispassionately at a situation and say 'That's the way it is,' but in relationships my head was too full of expectations and programming to see clearly."

If you want to boost your hit rate, begin by studying yourself.

Notice how your intuition communicates with you. Intuition seems to come in on three channels: word, picture, and body-sense. Most of us receive better on one channel than another, so it helps to find out what your best channel is. For example, think of a question like "Where do you want to be five years from now?" A word-channel response to this question might be a sentence flashing across the mind: "I want to be chief financial officer." A picture-channel response might be an image of yourself sitting in a particular office. The body-sense channel might be a warm, pleasant sensation in your abdomen that carries with it a meaning, the good feeling of success.

No channel is better than any other; they all come from the same place—the intuitive capability that we all seem to be born with. You just need to find out where your strong channel is.

In helping several thousand people improve their intuition, we've noticed that the majority get their intuitions in the form of pictures and gut feelings rather than on the word-channel. Everybody's a little different, though, so you have to do some research inside yourself to find out. Check it out right now: Take ten seconds to imagine yourself at your most successful in your career. When you imagine yourself that way, do you see a picture in your mind or get a feeling in your body? Do you see or hear some words?

Now go to a finer level of detail. If you saw a picture, where did it occur? If you got a body-feeling, where did it occur? If you received words, where did they appear in your mind? Listen to a description from a highly intuitive person: "My most accurate intuitions seem to happen about one-quarter to one-half inch to the right of the area between my eyes. The ones that aren't accurate seem to come from behind and to the left of that place." By zeroing in on the body location of your intuition, you get a clearer sense of where to go for the best information.

Once you're familiar with your inner patterns, start to practice on everyday events. In our Integrity/Vision trainings we practice intuition-sharpening exercises with real-life experiments that give immediate feedback. For example, we tune in to weather changes and fluctuations in the price of gold, coffee, and other commodities that bounce around a lot in price. Often by the end of the training, people are predicting rain, sunshine, and price movements with unerring accuracy.

Kate has used intuition from the beginning of her business career, and she has also interviewed many Corporate Mystics to learn their secrets: "I have always been fascinated by the ability to see the future accurately. By 1981 I had begun to do everything I could to increase my intuition, so I decided to set up personal practices and experiments that would help me learn.

"In the early eighties my office was in a magnificent old building in San Francisco. I worked on the second floor, while many of the managers I worked with were on the eighth floor. This meant I spent a lot of time waiting in front of a bank of six elevators. Putting this time to good use, I began checking inside to let my intuition tell me which elevator to stand in front of. When I started I was right about half the time, but within several months my elevator hunches were proving right nine out of ten times. This let me know that intuition was something that could be learned, sharpened, and improved experimentally. One week I went twenty times without an error.

"As my intuition got stronger, so did my trust in it. Although there had never been a layoff at this company, and the CEO had said publicly many times there never would be one, my intuition told me differently. I began spontaneously to think of how a layoff could be handled gracefully and to develop ideas about the implementation of one. On the surface these speculations seemed totally out of sync with reality, until one lunchtime. This day I had a hunch not to go out to lunch (a no-lunch hunch?), but to stay at my desk. Out of the blue the CEO dropped into my office, which he had rarely done, and told me that there would need to be a 40 percent layoff. He asked me if I had any ideas on how best to proceed! Without blinking I gave him a whole plan, with accompanying organizational diagrams. Needless to say, my stock rose in the company."

BECOMING BIGGER THAN THE PROBLEM

When Bob Marshall took over as CEO at Silicon Optics, he was faced with a crisis his first month. Practically the first piece of paper put in his hand was a report saying that a major new product, a piece of technology he had been hired to shepherd into the market, was not working as it should and that nobody knew how to make it work.

Bob recollects: "At first my head was swimming. This was about the worst news I could imagine. Fortunately I hadn't had to relocate my family, so I had the freedom of treating it purely as a business problem. But what should I do? Leave? Stay? Bring in consultants? Because I'd had training in the use of intuition at my previous company, I shut the door and asked that my calls be held for an hour. As it happened, I didn't even need the whole hour.

"I put my feet up and got comfortable. For a few minutes I just closed my eyes and let myself feel all the emotions pouring through my body. I did my best not to resist or censor them. Anger at the board... fear that I'd been lied to... fear that my career was about to take a plunge... fear that I wouldn't be able to pull it out... fear about what my wife would think when I told her I might be out of a job... After a few minutes my mind and body settled down, and I began counting my breaths to get very still inside.

"When I got into the quiet place inside, I posed a simple question: What was the best course of action to take at this time? I asked the question and let go of any need to answer it. I just got receptive and let the images come. I'm strong on the visual-channel, and I saw a clear path open up, just like I was looking at a photo slide of a clearly marked path through difficult terrain. My next question was: What's the first step? Quick as lightning, a piece of information appeared in my mind: It said 'Be a listener.' It came in on the word-channel, a sentence that said 'Listen to yourself and listen to them.' As I tuned in further, the sense of the message was that I needed to be absolutely truthful with myself and everybody else, particularly the board. I saw in my mind that as long as I behaved with impeccability I had nothing to fear.

"The whole process took less than fifteen minutes, and I came out feeling great. I still had all the same issues to face, but suddenly everything had changed. Now I knew I was bigger than the problem was."

The upshot was that Bob met with the board, aired all his feelings, and listened while they aired theirs. He went into the meeting with a little piece of paper he kept in front of him the entire time. It said, "Listen to myself and listen to them." At the end of the meeting the board decided to fold the project and scale down, which meant hiring a much less expensive person than Bob. They cut him a check for $100,000 in severance, and he went back to work for his former company, where he is now CEO. Interviewed a few years later, he said, "Intuition really saved the day for me. I could have gotten into a loop with the board, making them wrong and duking it out with them. Or I could have stewed in the whole situation for a year and driven myself crazy. Instead, by listening to myself and them, by following my intuition, I got out cleanly. The clear path turned out to take me back to where I'd been, to my old company. But while I'd been away they found out how much they missed me. I don't think I could have become CEO without that few months over at Silicon Optics."

> *It is always with excitement that I wake up in the morning wondering what my intuition will toss up to me, like gifts from the sea. I work with it and rely upon it. It's my partner.*
>
> —Dr. Jonas Salk

DEVELOPING GOOD PEOPLE-INTUITION

Have you noticed that some people—maybe a manager, a teacher, or a friend—seem to be able to read your mind? Somehow their sensory radar seems to work better than other people's. Although some people may be gifted in this area, we know for sure that people-intuition can also be learned. The real problem is not in learning a new skill but in learning how not to overlook what you've been seeing all along. People are organically intuitive; we come factory-equipped that way. In fact, it takes effort not to be intuitive.

Here's how we learn not to be intuitive. Let's say that one day early in your career you notice that your boss looks uncomfortable when he talks about last month's sales figures. You, in your unpolished enthusiasm, blurt out: "I notice you looked uncomfortable when you talked about the sales figures. What's up?" If people are open and in a good mood, they often receive these kinds of communications readily, even gratefully. But let's say your boss is mad about the sales figures and decides to take it out on you. He blasts you and tells you to worry about your performance, not how he looks.

These kinds of events first happen in childhood, where we are asked or forced to overlook things we see to preserve the status quo. In our Integrity/Vision trainings, we find that in a roomful of fifty people as many as thirty will remember experiences of being punished for some intuition, hunch, or observation they shared as a child. Sometimes it only takes one negative experience to snuff out our inborn sense of intuition. On the positive side, human beings are famous for their resilience, so it is possible to overcome these early learnings and give your intuition room to flourish again.

A CEO client of Kate's tells a remarkable story about the power of people-intuition: "We were in a complex negotiation worth hundreds of millions of dollars. We were stalled out, about $75 million apart, and everyone was getting tremendously frustrated. Finally, we called time-out and took a break to reflect. During the break it occurred to us that the issue didn't have anything to do with the technical aspects of the deal. It was really about the other side wondering if we liked them. We were trying to pour on more and more details, when it was actually an emotional issue. So, when we got back together we focused in on how much we liked them and wanted to work with them. The deal was resolved very shortly."

Intuitive managers have special skills that are likely to become more valuable in tomorrow's rapidly changing environment. They are likely to be the people who dream up the new products of tomorrow. They are the people who have a feel for what the consumer wants and how much he or she is willing to pay for it.

—Weston Agor

INTUITIVE HIRING

Lou Ann Scardino, vice-president of a cosmetics firm, made a key personnel decision using her intuition, one that later proved to be accurate and highly profitable: "We needed a new leader for our new-products division. We interviewed half a dozen people and narrowed it down to two. They were both highly qualified but about as different as two people could be. Larry was articulate, handsome, and a charmer, down to the cuff links and the Armani suit. He also had a fine track record with another company, so it was clear that he wasn't just appearances. Andy, who had worked for our company for years in a different division, always dressed like he was put together by a committee. He looked like a grown-up Goofy the Dog, a bit of a bumbler. I had many conscious considerations about both of them, but what finally helped me was using my intuition.

"One Sunday afternoon at home, I took a glass of wine out on the patio and spent a few minutes opening up my intuition to solve the problem. I centered myself and posed the question, "Which of these two guys would be best for the company?" It was fascinating and somewhat scary, because every time I tuned in to Larry, I got alarm signals and physical pains in my body, like someone screeching chalk on a chalkboard. When I tuned in to Andy, I felt calm and centered, and I had images of what a calming influence he would be on the team.

"Monday I made the decision and gave the job to Andy. At the same time I offered Larry another position in one of our marketing divisions. He took it and things went well for about two months. Then he got embroiled in a difficult divorce and his performance went downhill very rapidly. He got a DUI ticket, then another one which resulted in losing his license. We let him go and got him into a treatment program. I have since heard that he has changed careers and become a drug and alcohol counselor. Andy is doing extremely well as team leader. My big regret is that I didn't listen to my intuition all the way, which would have probably meant not offering Larry any sort of job. I think my personal response to his charms clouded my ability to trust my intuition completely."

FEAR CLOUDS INTUITION

Intuition must be nurtured. At first, it is important simply to uncover it so that it can live and breathe. Since intuition is wired in, a natural gift, nothing has to be attained in order to be more intuitive. Rather, the process is one of clearing away the things that block its use and appreciation. Fear is the main thing that must be cleared away.

Fear breeds projection, a killer of intuition. We know, for example, that several hundred people rushing toward O'Hare Airport on any given morning may have pictures of their airplanes crashing. Almost never do these "flashes" turn out to be valid intuitions. These images come from their own personal fears and are being projected onto the airplane flight.

As you work to sharpen your intuition, learn to distinguish the voice of fear from the voice of intuition. You might have a thought of not going to New York for a sales call. Is this thought coming from a fear that you won't be able to make the sale? Or is it a genuine intuition that your trip will be unproductive? There is only one way to find out: Acknowledge your fears first. Find out how your fear-thoughts look and feel, and learn to appreciate the difference between them and genuine intuitive hits. It takes practice.

Businesspeople often suffer from a particular fear that limits their creativity and intuition. To put it bluntly, it is the fear of looking foolish. Let's face it: We've all embarrassed ourselves at least a few times in our lives. This implants a fear of looking like a fool deep in our bodies. Anybody who has passed through the educational system has many years of training in trying not to look foolish.

To access creativity and intuition, we must drive out this fear. Fear keeps us trapped in the realm of the predictable. While we are in thrall to the fear of looking ridiculous, our colleagues who have cleared up this fear are busily designing new equipment, dreaming up outrageous campaigns, and coming up with ingenious personnel assignments. Sure, some of their designs and campaigns may look stupid and prove utterly unworkable. When this happens, they just take a deep breath and go back to the drawing boards.

> *The greatest advances in man's understanding of the universe are made by intuitive leaps at the frontiers of knowledge, not by intellectual walks along well-travelled paths.*
>
> —ANDREW WEIL, M.D.

A company president told us: "When I get stuck, I like to leaf through the notebooks of Leonardo da Vinci. Many of his designs were totally ridiculous and still are. But some of his inventions were ridiculous only in the context of his time. His designs for the parachute and the helicopter were basically correct, although they were five hundred years ahead of their time. What I respect, though, is that his commitment to his creativity was bigger than his fear of looking stupid. He was willing to play with his creativity, a sure sign of mastery."

To get to the zone of intuition many people have to walk through the gate of another fear: being crazy. Some people are afraid to open up to the unknown in themselves, for fear that some monster slumbers deep within. Some of us grew up around people whose intuitiveness became mingled with irrational acts, so that later we came to resist intuition because we feared our own inner voices. Both of the authors had family members or acquaintances who fit this category. Gay: "As my paternal grandmother slid into senile dementia, her telepathic abilities increased in direct proportion to her paranoid fantasies. Sometimes she would get a great intuitive hit and predict the arrival of a letter from a distant relative. These accurate intuitions were mixed up with wildly crazy ones, like her conviction that my mother was having an affair with Franklin Delano Roosevelt. I think this gave the whole family a fear of the intuitive." Kate: "I had a neighbor who was lobotomized when I was growing up, and that gave me a fear of what might happen if I opened up to my inner voices. Also, children's books were full of witch archetypes, which didn't inspire little girls to open up to their magical powers."

If you discover any of these fears, understand that they are normal and natural. Many people have had to move through them in order to get on a congenial basis with their intuition. Just as jumping in the water the first time can be scary, so can a jump into the vast ocean of your intuitive powers. Once you get comfortable there, some real and useful pleasure can be yours.

REMOVING THE INNER CRITIC

Most of us by adulthood have acquired a severe inner critic and an internal hanging judge. These mental marionette masters keep us frozen or jumping through hoops not of our own conscious choosing. There is only one way to acquire the judge and critic: Somebody told us there was something fundamentally wrong with us. We were wrong because we were the wrong color, the wrong sex, the wrong socioeconomic class. Even if you've risen above this, you can still have remnants of it buried deep in your cells. You might feel that acknowledging a mistake is the same as acknowledging that there is something fundamentally bad about your being itself. Nobody likes to face that, so we often defend ourselves against it by needing to be right all the time.

In our consultations with executives, we have often seen great breakthroughs in leadership come when they are able to let go of the need to be right. Letting go of the need to be right is also crucial to turning on the power of intuition. Intuition is best accessed with a nonjudgmental mind, a mind that says, "Let me just take what I get from my intuitive depths as it comes, and I'll evaluate, judge, and edit later." This is a correct use of the judging and evaluating mind.

Intuition often turns dreams into demonstrable facts.

—BUCKMINSTER FULLER

WHAT WE FEAR IS OUR OWN POWER

The dominant human fear is the fear of the unknown. It can severely limit your ability to open up to your intuition. This fear causes us to live in the zone of complacency, where creativity and intuition do not dwell. As long as we are in the grip of the fear of the unknown, no great leaps of mind are possible.

When we fear the unknown, what we are really fearing is the depths and heights of our own power. If we open up and connect with the powerful creativity of our intuitive mind, we are at once opening to the creative power of the universe that resides in microcosm within us. This is strong stuff, so strong that there is a widespread tendency to avoid contact with this creative potential. We delude ourselves into thinking that it is safer to stay in the zone of the predictable. This, however, can be a bad bargain, especially if we want to go all the way to full success in life. The moment we choose to stay in the predictable zone is the moment we sign our death warrant as a creative individual.

We also fear the great responsibility that goes along with great power. The intuitive is our connection with our ability to make and remake the world. We may have an intuitive flash of how the atom is constructed, but along with it comes a sense of responsibility for how this knowledge might be used. Instead of resisting our intuitive powers and resisting the responsibility, the mystic embraces both.

INTUITION IS A PHENOMENON OF THE GAP

Intuition dwells in the gap between ordinary thoughts. Much of the time our thoughts seem jumbled together so tightly that there doesn't seem to be any space between them. But if you look carefully, you will see that there is open space between and behind all your thoughts. Intuition occurs in this gap.

The gap is the province of the mystic. Mystics are comfortable in the gap, while non-mystics experience fear when they're there. Non-mystics are comfortable only in the predictable territory of their known thoughts. Mystics cannot live in the zone of the known for very long without feeling stultified. To find intuition and make it your friend, you must enter the gap.

> *The gaps are the thing. The gaps are the spirit's one home, the altitudes and latitudes so dazzlingly spare and clean that the spirit can discover itself like a once-blind man unbound.*
>
> —ANNIE DILLARD

There are formal ways to enter the gap, such as through meditation. Part Three of this book contains a short, effective means of entering the gap and turning on your intuition. There are also informal ways to access the gap. The simplest way is to pose a question, then let go of the need to have an answer right away. It is a seeding technique; you sow the question, then let go of it to await the surprise of an answer later.

As an experiment right now, pose a question that has significance for you. Just ask it in your mind and let go of it. If you notice, the question is surrounded and embraced by a vast space. That's the gap. Just relax into it and get comfortable there. That's the comfort zone of the mystic: the friendly unknown, the zone of all possibilities. From somewhere in the gap, when the time is right, you may be surprised by an answer to your question.

CONTROL CRAMPS INTUITION

If you want to live in the zone of intuition rather than just visit it, cultivate the skill of letting go of control. This skill is difficult for businesspeople, who often think they have gotten where they are through their ability to control. But to go all the way to full success, you have to master controlling what is controllable and letting go of everything outside your control. There is a specific way to do this.

Imagine you have two boxes. Box 1 is labeled "Things over which I have absolutely no control." Box 2 is labeled "Things over which I have complete control." Mystics learn to assign all the elements of life to the correct box and to then focus all their attention on Box 2.

Box 1 is surprisingly large, and gets larger the more you think about it. Among the things you cannot control are:

- The feelings and actions of other people.
- Anything that has already happened—the past.
- Anything that hasn't happened yet—the future.
- Most of what goes on inside your own body.

You cannot control other people, the past, or the future. But what about that last item on the list? Many people think they can control what goes on inside their bodies. Forget about controlling your poor liver, which every minute is doing several hundred things, most of which are unpronounceable. Think about controlling your feelings. Imagine being afraid just before making a speech. If you had control over your fear you would be able to make it go away. And we all know how well that works. That's why the wise mystic counsels: When you're feeling scared (or angry or sad), simply acknowledge it, resonate with it, tell the truth about it. Trying to control it is like squeezing the middle of a garden hose while water is flowing through it.

Or consider your weight. Even the most perfect physical specimen has no control over his or her weight. Don't believe it? Go step on the scales and check your weight. Then try to make it go up or down. Did it? No. You have no control over it. But what do you have control over? What can you put in Box 2? You have complete control over what you put in your mouth. You have complete control over whether you get up right now and get on your exercise bike. What you can control and what you cannot: It's a key distinction. The mystic focuses on what can be controlled and accepts the rest just as it is. From this deep acceptance of reality, exactly as it is, comes the possibility of choosing to make it different.

Relationships with other people? That's where we really come up against our lack of control. The harder you try the worse it gets. Just ask any former despot. Mao once had everyone in China reading his Little Red Book, to convince the citizens of the superiority of communism over capitalism; now the book is a novelty item, found in the souvenir shops along the Great Wall. Mao's picture is widely available on T-shirts, which the Chinese are very happy to trade for capitalist blue jeans.

The mystic knows the difference between control and influence. While you cannot control other people, the past, the future, or much of anything about yourself, you can certainly influence them. Control comes out of fear; influence is exercised consciously with a goal and a plan. Control is the offspring of desperation; influence is carried out in a businesslike fashion.

Letting go of control is the first step; it frees up the energy you will need. There is a simple, powerful strategy for dealing with all the contents of Box 1, the things you cannot control. Face them and accept them, just as they are. Many people tie up all their energy in resistance to things they cannot change. This same energy, freed up, is the stuff that fuels miracles.

> *You can't control most things in the outside world,*
> *but you can control yourself.*
> *When things are going wrong,*
> *the best thing you can do is focus inward*
> *and question what you can do differently*
> *or how you messed it up*
> *rather than blaming things you can't control.*
>
> —BRIAN SHARPLES,
> FOUNDER AND FORMER CEO, HOMEAWAY

THREE MILLION DOLLARS' WORTH OF INTUITION

Kate, who describes herself as a very risk-aversive person, used intuition to deal with her fear of risk and start an enterprise that has since yielded an impressive payoff: "I took January 1991 off for rest and relaxation, as a reward for my first year of billing half a million dollars as a consultant. I spent most of it with my daughter, enjoying the outdoors. For a year I had been toying with the idea of creating proprietary software for conducting personnel assessments and other surveys. Every time I thought about this I got the special flurrying feeling in my chest that I get when I have an intuition that I ought to move on rapidly. The glitch was that these developmental projects are costly, and I would have to dig deep into my own pocket to do it. Also, I talked to several companies to assess enthusiasm for 360-degree assessments. It was lukewarm at best, because no one knew that such assessments would become popular until a few years later.

"I decided to run the idea past Ken Schroeder, president of KLA Instruments, who had been a mentor and coach to me in the mid-eighties. Ken strongly recommended that I go ahead. I mounted some resistance, arguing that my daughter was just starting college and I didn't have extra money to spend. In spite of what my inner critic said, I trusted Ken, and I trusted my own body-sense of intuition. Even though I had little support from my potential customers I decided to go ahead with the project. I spent $20,000 in 1991 on developing the product. After I had committed my own money and time, Intel gave me $15,000 to customize the software for their company, so in actuality I invested only $5,000 of my own money. To date, the product has brought in $3,000,000 in revenue. I'm tremendously grateful to Ken for helping me believe in the project and my own intuition."

Never lose a holy curiosity.

—Albert Einstein

PART TWO

THE PRACTICAL MYSTIC: SPIRITED SOLUTIONS TO EVERYDAY BUSINESS PROBLEMS

> *Manifest plainness,*
> *embrace simplicity.*
>
> —LAO-TZU

In this part we will present solutions Corporate Mystics have applied to some of the most common business problems we have encountered in our twenty-five years of consulting. These examples all show mystics at work, drawing on the principles of integrity, vision, and intuition. In our travels we have seen four main areas in which problems occur.

The first area is commitment. When people are not committed, little productivity is possible. The cultures of many corporations are cultures of non-commitment. There is entitlement, apathy, and downright sabotage at work in some of the largest and oldest companies we have visited. In order to turn these companies around, radical work had to be done in the area of commitment.

Communication is the second area, and a large one it is. No matter how many books are written about communication in corporate settings, we keep seeing the same old communication breakdowns over and over again. As one of our frustrated colleagues put it at the end of a long meeting, "The level of communication in most corporations is approximately equal to that of the average junior high school. And that may be generous to corporations and an insult to junior high school students." What is really required is courageous practice of certain fundamental communication principles, and we have laid out the principles that we have seen to be of most benefit.

The third area is in managing projects. In any dynamic human enterprise there are going to be unexpected twists and turns. In fact, corporate life is a daily experience of the unexpected. It is likely to become more so in the twenty-first century. What will distinguish successful companies, perhaps more than anything else, will be a comfort and even enthusiasm for change, coupled with a reliable way of handling the unexpected.

The fourth area is the creation of wealth. While most people do not work only for money, they seldom work without it. Most people in corporate life are concerned with creating wealth for themselves and for others. In our consulting work, we have had the opportunity to ask many self-made millionaires how they went about creating wealth. They have shared a cornucopia of ideas with us, and while these principles are intrinsically fascinating, their cash value is that they work. We have personally tried each of the tools described in this section, and our wealth has increased as a direct result.

*In our era,
the road to holiness
necessarily passes through
the world of action.*

—DAG HAMMARSKJÖLD

4

INSPIRING COMMITMENT

Five frogs sat on a log. One decided to jump. How many frogs were left? Five. There's a big difference between deciding to jump and actually jumping. The inspired leader knows how to get total commitment, so that no frogs are left on the corporate log. Zero-frog leadership.

Getting "buy-in" is essential in every area of life: family, play, work. Have you ever tried to play a game—whether tennis, business, or marriage—with a partner who didn't really want to be there? All it takes to destroy a game is one person on the team who doesn't want to play.

A multimillion-dollar failure shows what can happen when buy-in is overlooked. We came in on the tail end of this fiasco to attempt a bailout, but by then it was too late. Because it was such a costly failure for the company, we took pains to "backward-map" the various steps that had led to the debacle. Here's what happened.

A new venture was put together within one of America's largest communication companies. A brilliant innovator had designed a new telecommunications product. Speed was of the essence because the technology was also under development in at least two other firms. The financial side of the house promised an eighteen-month deadline to the people who were funding the project. When the managers went to the creative people who would actually build the product and get it out the door, the eighteen-month deadline was greeted with derision. "No way" was the basic message.

Under this resistance were several layers of fear: the fear of losing jobs, the fear of being away from families for evenings and weekends, the fear of being in an adversarial relationship with management. Management, in their zeal to develop the product, overrode this resistance heavy-handedly, offering promises of great rewards if the deadline was met. The resistance went underground. The one misstep that seemed crucial in retrospect was that the feelings of all concerned never got an airing. Everyone gave lip service to the deadline, but the design team never fully got on board.

A sense of mistrust soon permeated the project. Everyone had both a public and a private version of their feelings. The main topic of whispered conversations in the lunchroom was the Deadline. Eighteen-hour days and six-day weeks became the norm, with many people coming in on Sunday afternoons. Finally, everything came to a head a couple of months before the deadline, in the form of an emotional blowup between the head of the design team and the head of the financial side of the company. Everyone's feelings came pouring out in the kind of messy confrontation that engineers, especially, do not relish. The deadline was exposed as unfeasible, threats were made, three people went home sick.

From then on, a pall lingered in the air, which cleared only when a new deadline was set, with a five-month extension. Meanwhile, Company B delivered a version of the product to market a few months early and soon dominated the field. Company A brought theirs in under the new deadline, but by then the energy was dead.

All of this could have been avoided. The rest of the chapter shows you how.

RECOGNIZING THE MOST COMMON COMMITMENT PROBLEM

As consultants, the commitment problem we have seen more than any other is this: People do not buy in to a project, assignment, or vision. The leader does not perceive this lack of buy-in, or chooses to ignore it. Instead of speaking up and voicing whatever the resistance is, people swallow their communication and act as if they have bought in. They file dutifully out of the meeting, and then the troubles begin. They passively resist, perhaps not completing work on time. They gossip about the project or the leader or the people who have bought in. All of the problems have stemmed from a lack of up-front commitment.

A related problem is that people will make an agreement, perhaps to meet a certain deadline. Some event, often outside their control, will get in the way, and they won't know how to change the agreement. Feet will be dragged, sick days will be taken, the project delayed.

The solution is obvious but not easy to implement. Leaders have to get skilled at recognizing the signals of noncommitment. The best way is to watch body language. Notice the averted eyes, the glance at the watch, obsessive fiddling with the coffee cup. There are dozens of ways people telegraph their feelings. The savvy leader must be willing to find out what is behind these fidgets.

"Bill, I notice when we set the deadline you looked uncomfortable. I'd really like to know how you actually feel about it." These can be tough moments for leaders, who often want to hear what they want to hear. In these moments people might be feeling:

- Fear that they won't be able to deliver.
- Anxious that resources won't be available.
- Fear that a time-consuming project will disrupt family life.

The important thing for leaders is to look for signs of noncommitment in the first moments and hear people out. It is also important to create a climate in which people can talk about their authentic feelings without fearing punishment. Timing is often crucial in such confrontations. Some people do not like to speak out in meetings; they can be contacted later over a cup of coffee. Sensitive leaders study the styles of their key people so that an effective avenue of approach can be designed for each person.

An ounce of this sort of attention up front can prevent a ton of problems later on.

KNOWING YOUR PURPOSE

Your first step in getting commitment is to know your ultimate purpose. It is hard to inspire commitment unless you can speak your purpose in one clear sentence. It is hard to get committed to something if you don't know what it is. It is hard to get others committed if they're not sure of what they're committing to. One thing you have absolute control over in life is where to put your focus.

Members of a Yale graduating class in the 1950s were surveyed periodically throughout their lives to assess their well-being, happiness, and financial abundance. All of them were bright, many of them were wealthy. But 3 percent of them had an edge that later proved significant. When first contacted, 3 percent of them had developed written goals for their lives as they left college. Thirty years later that 3 percent was worth more money than the other 97 percent put together.

Purpose.

What you most want.

If you figure out your purpose you won't wander aimlessly and you won't settle for side steps that take you away from your purpose. Without a clear sense of your purpose there are a thousand and one sidetracks to seduce you. A great advantage of knowing your purpose is that it becomes easier to make decisions. You know at a glance whether a specific path serves your purpose or not. Many people, in a misguided attempt to keep more options open, fail to make clean decisions and suffer for it.

THE PURPOSE OF PURPOSE

There are Big Life Purposes and there are small daily purposes. Both are equally important. The function of both is to give shape and definition to your actions.

Your Big Life Purpose is the answer to questions like: What, above all, am I really here for? What do I most love to do? At the end of my life, if it had been a total success, what would I have experienced and accomplished?

Small daily purposes are the answer to questions like: What do we want to accomplish with this project? What spirit do we want to lend to this enterprise? What feelings and accomplishments do I want to walk away from this meeting with? What emotional state do I want to be in as I go about my tasks?

An inspiring leader knows how to connect the small, incremental (and often irksome) steps with the Big Vision. When you see someone doing a trivial but essential job, pause by the person's desk and say, "I appreciate the care you're giving this job. It's obvious you remember the purpose, why we're all doing this."

There needs to be harmony between your Big Life Purposes and your daily purposes for you to be happy. If there is conflict between the two, expect rattles and bumps along the journey.

INTEGRITY IS CENTRAL TO COMMITMENT

Nothing deflates commitment faster than broken agreements. One broken promise can erode trust in a moment, and can take years to straighten out. If you really want to complicate your life quickly, don't keep your agreements. At the bottom of most corporate disasters is a small pile of broken agreements. Sometimes just one. If you break an agreement and show up a minute late for a meeting, others will use this as justification to steal paper clips. Someone will see them stealing paper clips and get inspired to embezzle the pension fund.

Deadlines are a kind of agreement that is worth paying careful attention to. Deadlines are crucial to corporate life. The mystic solution to deadlines is: Never make a deadline you don't intend to keep. People get sloppy when deadlines are extended or swept under the rug. Don't let people in your organization waste a second trying to figure out if a deadline is real or not. If you don't mean it, don't do it.

The rules are simple: Don't make agreements you don't want to make. Keep all the agreements you make. Tell the rock-bottom truth if you find you are not going to keep an agreement. Cop to it immediately if you fail to keep an agreement.

Hold yourself responsible for a higher standard than anyone else expects of you.

—HENRY WARD BEECHER

DOING WHAT NEEDS TO BE DONE

How many people do you know who can be counted on to do what they say they are going to do? If they were counting, would they count you? Pros are people who can keep showing up day after day, doing a good job even when they don't feel like it.

How do you know what most needs to be done? Look and see. Ask. On the battlefield, doctors use the art and science of triage: They separate the wounded into three categories. The first category are those who are going to live, with or without medical treatment. The second category are those who are going to die, with or without treatment. The third category are those who will die unless they receive treatment. The last category gets the priority on the doctors' efforts. We have seen many executives benefit from developing a triage system for their daily activities. There are always paramount activities that will cost you and the company if not attended to. Too many executives waste time and energy on activities that are not crucial.

Corporate Mystics often employ a trick: They do the thing they would least like to do first. Then the rest of the day is like vacation. Who are you most dreading talking to? What decision are you painfully aware that you haven't made yet, but which absolutely needs to be made? Whose phone message keeps staring you in the face?

Everything begins with a commitment. In the beginning was the word. There is a tiny club that truly deserves to be elite: those people that know what their purpose is and who can be counted on to do what they say they are going to do.

Sit, walk, or run.
Just don't wobble.

—ZEN SAYING

WHY PEOPLE DON'T HONOR THEIR COMMITMENTS

The moment you make a commitment, you are pulled rapidly in the direction of your goal. This increased velocity brings to the surface your barriers to being completely effective. If you make big commitments, you will often face big barriers. If you ever find yourself thinking "I didn't ask for this kind of trouble!" just look back at your commitments. You will often see that big barriers follow hot on the heels of big commitments.

There are three barriers that most of us are likely to encounter. The first is wrong information. If we are misinformed about ourselves, others, or the world, making a big commitment will usually expose where our errors lie. Not long ago, a bright, young star ascended to a corporate presidency. He was articulate, hardworking, and charismatic. Soon, corridors were buzzing with the rumor that the president was having an affair with another charismatic young star, a vice-president in the organization. The corporate culture had a taboo against such relationships; the new president chose to stonewall, denying there was anything more than a friendship. In doing this, he fell prey to a fatal piece of misinformation: that no one notices when you sweep a lie under the rug. The more he denied, the bigger the uproar got. Finally, he was forced out and quickly revealed his hand by marrying the woman.

In analyzing this situation, we would say that his ascendance to the presidency was a deeper commitment on his part. At the higher level, which surely represented a lifetime dream of his, everything was required of him. The deeper commitment exposed the flaw that he had been able to conceal or manage at lower levels of commitment.

Now let's turn to the second barrier.

HANDLING FEAR, DOUBT, AND CONFUSION

The moment you declare a big commitment, another barrier may rise up to hinder you: uncomfortable feelings. Take, for example, the perennial problem of dieting. Millions of people every day make a commitment to follow a diet. Most diets fail for a simple and powerful reason. Within minutes perhaps, certainly within hours, they are feeling uncomfortable emotions like fear and hunger. These are the very same feelings that their bad eating habits are designed to squelch. The only way to make a diet succeed is to handle those feelings, perhaps by experiencing them deeply, breathing through them, going for a run. Unwilling to be with these feelings, they eat their forbidden foods again. Unwillingness to go through the gate of uncomfortable emotions causes people to sabotage their commitments.

If you are doing anything big and worthwhile in life, you are going to flush up uncomfortable feelings. The bigger the commitment, the bigger the bundle of feelings that is likely to come up. Big commitments mean big wins and big losses. Both wins and losses stir up the pot of your feelings. The mystic knows that big commitments are often followed by big fears, doubts, and confusions. Imagine the feelings that must have surfaced as Columbus's ship lost sight of the European shore! Veteran Corporate Mystics know about the second barrier and give themselves and their co-workers plenty of opportunities to tell the truth about their feelings. They make a space of safety in which to feel all feelings, but keep everyone reminded that feelings pass through like gusts of wind. Feel whatever you feel, says the mystic, and keep focused on doing what needs to be done.

There's no choice about whether you are going to have the feelings; the only choice is how you are going to participate with them. The mystic knows that peace of mind flows from total participation, with fear, with sorrow, with joy. With feelings, all you can do is see them, feel them, and keep on moving. The worst thing you can do is deny them and hide them.

Once you have chosen a path and committed to it, regard all your doubts as noise. Fear plays a useful role only until you are committed: It is the energy of choice. Once you have committed, most fear will disappear. If any remains, regard it as a cue that you are not taking action fast enough.

MISPLACED LOYALTIES

When you make a deep commitment, a third barrier arises—misplaced loyalty—and it is often the most difficult to cross. The moment you declare, "My goal is to make $300,000 a year" or "I would like to have a loving marriage," you invariably expose the hidden bonds that keep you shackled to the past.

The mystic knows the power of invisible loyalties. For example, many people do not rise to the full level of their potential out of unconscious loyalty to a failed and wounded parent. It is for this reason that Corporate Mystics work carefully not to confuse their own personal story/dramas with what needs to be done. Everybody has their story/dramas: Some of us are betrayals waiting to happen, others of us are misunderstood geniuses, still others are hidden heroes afraid to take the leap. Regardless of whether your story is a comedy or a tragedy, it absolutely needs to be distinguished from what most needs to be done. These are two separate categories: your story, and what needs to be done in every given situation. Many of us sabotage our enterprises by getting our stories muddled up with what needs to be done.

Remember the young president who was having the affair? He got his own story/drama confused with what needed to be done. His story, based on his history with his authoritarian father, was about "How much can I get away with?" What he needed to do—lead the corporation—was to be authentic about his affair to the employees and the board, and to choose consciously between the love relationship and the presidency.

Corporate Mystics know that everyone's story is sacred to them, whether it is about betrayal or heroism. The Corporate Mystic's edge is being able to see how his or her story is clouding what needs to be done and to do what needs to be done anyway. If the mystic is a manager, he or she learns how to acknowledge people's stories but keep them focused on what needs to be done.

When we get confused about what needs to be done, it is often because we are in thrall to an ancient version of ourselves. The same is true for any organization. Corporations often stay fixated on a limited version of themselves. There are frequently loyalties to old visions, former leaders. Corporate Mystics confront this issue head-on. They ask: "Who are we being loyal to by not doing what needs to be done?"

RECOGNIZING AND REWARDING COMMITTED PEOPLE

Keeping people committed is a high art, part of which is finding ways to recognize their contributions. Money is the obvious way, but most people don't work for money alone. Creative leaders find ways of stepping into the shoes of other people and asking, "How would I feel and what would I want if I were this person?"

Bill Wiggenhorn, president of Motorola University, found a unique way of compensating a unique individual who reported to him. From his conversations with her he knew that money played a very small role in her life. She, in fact, lived simply and gave most of her money away to charity. He wanted to increase her compensation in a way that would recognize and benefit her, and he knew if he gave her more money it would not have that result. So, he stepped into her shoes and asked himself what he would want if he shared her spiritual values. More education and training, he thought. Instead of increasing her salary, he put aside funds for her professional development and offered her some flextime to pursue it. These contributions allowed her to complete her doctorate, which had been unfinished for several years.

> *Somebody ought to tell us,*
> *right at the start of our lives,*
> *that we are dying.*
> *Then we might live life*
> *to the limit every minute of every day.*
> *Do it! I say.*
> *Whatever you want to do,*
> *do it now.*
>
> —MICHAEL LANDON

5

COMMUNICATING WITH PEOPLE

Put your heart, mind, and soul into even your smallest acts. That is the secret of success.

—Swami Sivananda

Corporate Mystics know a secret: Genuine communication is possible only when you are fully present—being there, wherever you are. Mystics put their attention on their wandering attention, bringing it back to the present, here where I am.

At its best, work is play. When you are fully engaged, when your full capacities are in use and creativity is flowing, there is no such thing as work. Then you are just doing what you are doing. If you watch children at play—fully there, completely earnest, engaged—you will see the exact attitude that Corporate Mystics cultivate at work.

Jim Jarman took over the presidency of an undercapitalized biotech start-up on the West Coast: "My first week on the job I was confronted with a dizzying number of problems no one had told me about. Some were financial, others were technical, many were personality related. I remember playing with my daughter in the family room on Friday night after my first week of work. My daughter suddenly said, 'Where are you, Dad?' and I realized I was in a trance. I was nowhere near being where I was. In fact, I was running through my financing options for getting a cash infusion for the company. I felt guilty as heck for letting my work get in the way of my relationship with my daughter, so I got down on the floor with Andrea, who was in kindergarten at the time. 'Teach me how to play, honey. Show me how you play.' She didn't bat an eyelash. She grinned at me and said 'okay,' and for the next hour I got reacquainted with playing. I just did what she did, and when she went from one thing to the next I followed right with her. What I noticed was how she paid total attention to what she was doing. When she played with the dolls, she was right there with them, completely engaged. But when we switched to trucks, she gave her full attention to them. I saw that my mistake at work had been to go to the next activity while leaving part of my mind behind on the last one. Or farming out another part of my mind to the future. Andrea didn't do this at all. The secret of her play was that she was right where she was. When I went up to join my wife later, she asked me what I had been doing down there that had kept Andrea so engaged. 'She was teaching me how to do my new job,' I said.

"When I got back to work Monday I posted a sign on my wall that said, 'Remember Andrea's Secret.' Probably fifteen times that week somebody asked me what Andrea's secret was. And I told it over and over until I got it."

> *The secret of success is nonattachment to results;*
> *doing your best at the moment,*
> *and letting the results take care of themselves.*
>
> —J. DONALD WALTERS

BEING AUTHENTIC

Good communication starts at home, inside yourself. Is your communication with yourself clear and direct? One thing they don't teach us in school is how to listen to and honor all our feelings. It is left to life to teach us, often painfully, how to listen to the signals from our inner selves. One of the main messages of life is: Don't lie to yourself. Lying to others will get you in trouble, but lying to yourself will make you sick. And fast.

What are you pretending not to know?

—Graffiti in a Harvard Business
School Restroom

The problem becomes obvious when we are trying to communicate with others and they can clearly see we are not communicating with ourselves. Bluntly put, life gets painfully complicated the moment you lie to yourself or to someone else. Enlightened leaders tell the truth to themselves and the people around them. The Buddha said it plainly: Unhappiness comes from not facing some reality that you need to face squarely.

*The first step to becoming a leader is to
stop pretending, especially to ourselves.*

—An Anonymous Corporate Mystic

Sometimes this reality is inside, sometimes outside. Sometimes the reality is in the past, sometimes in the present. Kate worked with two vice-presidents who were locked in a power struggle: "The CFO of a high-tech company in Silicon Valley was a black man named Dan. A white woman, Gracie, was the vice-president of sales. They got into a communication breakdown so extreme that they would not even sit in a meeting together without a third party. After looking over the situation, I didn't think it was fixable. I suggested they both look at their individual stories that were contributing to the drama. The level of mistrust seemed way out of the norm. As we worked on their issues separately, suddenly she surfaced a memory of a traumatic early childhood experience with a relative of a black nanny she'd had when she was a child. As we got this sorted out, she found out that Dan was Dan, not some shadow figure from the past. On his end, he uncovered, an old program of white women being beyond his reach, and Gracie, who happened to be a "homecoming queen" beauty, seemed particularly annoying to him. Finally, he saw her as Grade, not as some archetype of an unavailable woman. Now they're good friends, out from their projections on each other."

*The most exhausting thing in life,
I have discovered, is insincerity.*

—Anne Morrow Lindbergh

*I noticed that when people weren't listening to me
it was usually because I wasn't telling the truth.*

—An Anonymous Corporate Mystic

PLAIN TALKING

If you make sure you're telling the truth, you won't ever have to worry about people listening to you. When people don't listen, it's usually because the speaker's got something else he or she is communicating besides the truth. Say only true things and keep it brief. Mystics are famous for not making small talk.

If you want one thing to focus on at all times, one thing that will guarantee happiness and success, focus on whether or not every word you say is the truth.

Facts first. Part of learning to tell the truth is getting the facts right. Instead of saying "The other day I was talking to Joe," just go ahead and say, "Tuesday morning I was talking to Joe." Instead of "I've been noticing a lessened commitment on your part, Harvey," give him some facts. Say, "Harvey, you reported late on project A and you missed our Wednesday meeting on project B." A lot of people like to put a little spin on their facts, and it costs them their credibility. So, focus first on telling the truth about facts.

Then, make sure you tell the truth about feelings. If you're angry, don't try to hide it. People can see it anyway. Say, "I'm angry." If you're sad or disappointed, say it right out. Same thing for fear. A lot of people think feelings are a sign of weakness, but the truth is, they're a sign of being human. Nothing gives a leader more power than admitting to having feelings. Hiding your feelings makes you look bad and it throws your timing off. That doesn't mean you have to wallow in them or make a drama out of them. Mystics acknowledge and express their feelings the same way they acknowledge and express the time of day. Then they move on.

Any man who doesn't cry scares me a little bit.

—H. Norman Schwarzkopf

GET OUT OF THE MIDDLE

When we asked Corporate Mystics what their number one learning had been in the area of communication, many of them said: getting out of the middle. What they meant is this: Bob comes to you with a complaint about Marsha. You immediately ask, "Have you talked to Marsha about this?" Bob says he hasn't. "Go talk to her now. Come back later and give me a report." Many problems can be eliminated by getting out of the middle. If you are willing and have time, you can also say, "I'll call her in right now and we can all discuss it together." Either way saves much time and trouble down the line. It gets you out of perpetuating one of the oldest family dramas humans run. Many of us grew up in families where there was not straightforward communication. Mom would get upset at Dad but would filter it through Brother or Sister. Dad would be mad at Billy, who wouldn't find out until Mom told him. Roundabout communication costs a great deal of energy in human life, and there is only one efficient way to stop it. When it's your turn to play, don't.

I had to learn to ask questions
in a way where I showed that I understood,
psychologically, what's driving the other person.
There's a deeper way of learning how to ask questions.

—Arnold Donald,
CEO, Carnival Cruises

LISTENING FOR ACCURACY

Power lives more in listening than in talking. In fact, listening may be the key skill of the successful person. As soon as people feel that they've been listened to, they begin to evolve. They may have been stuck in one position for a long time, but a little bit of listening lubricates the hinge. As consultants, we have taught listening skills to thousands of people and have seen these skills work outright miracles. Take a moment now to ask yourself the question: How do you listen?

There are three levels to the development of listening skills. The first simple step is to feed back to people exactly what they said. This type of listening could be called "listening for accuracy."

Person A, beating on table with fist: "I want the Brooklyn Bridge and the Tappan Zee, or there's no deal."

Person B, a Corporate Mystic: "So you're saying you want the Brooklyn Bridge and the Tappan Zee, or there's no deal."

You might think such a response would come across sounding stupid. It does not. Try it and you will see what a radical move it is. People, especially when they have strong feelings, are so caught up in their own point of view that they are listening for opposition. It completely disarms them when you refuse to play. There is an electric moment of possibility when you listen to another human being with no agenda, no wanting them to see it your way. Pure listening. The Corporate Mystic thrives on such moments.

> *I always thought I was listening,*
> *but now I realize I have been just watching people's*
> *mouths move, waiting for them to stop so I could talk!*
>
> —Participant in a Seminar on Listening

A corporate officer told us: "I never knew the power of pure listening until one day a few years ago. There was a guy that I didn't get along with very well, partly because I had him labeled as a whiner. He bugged me because he seemed to recycle the same upset feelings all the time, particularly his feelings of competitiveness with other people at his level. One day we were having coffee in the cafeteria when he started again. I felt my gut tighten and my blood pressure start to go up. I had just read a book and listened to a tape on listening, though, so I decided to practice on him. Instead of agreeing with him or talking him out of his point of view, I simply restated it. I said, 'You're mad about Hilda getting a bigger salary increase, and you have a strong desire to move ahead in this company.' I did my best to say it with no judgment implied or expressed. After I said this, there was a silence. Finally, he said, 'Yeah,' and that was the end of it. He started talking about something much more pleasant. I don't know to this day if he stopped complaining in general or just to me, but I know for certain that I haven't heard him talk the same way since."

On a humorous note, a friend of the authors' went with his wife to a party where he knew almost no one. He decided to try an experiment: Rather than talking or trying to impress anyone at the party, he vowed to do nothing all evening but listen carefully and restate what each person said to him. On the way home his wife, glowing with pride, told him that several people had remarked about what a powerful, charismatic, and articulate person he was.

The first stage of learning to listen, then, is being able to summarize the content of what you've heard, just the way they said it. Teachers of listening will tell you that it takes about ten minutes to learn this skill and about ten years to master it.

LISTENING FOR EMPATHY

The second stage of learning to listen is to resonate with what the other person is saying, particularly the emotional content. We'll call this "listening for empathy." You do this by trying their emotions on in your own body. The other person says: "I want this company to be the industry leader in quality microchips by the year 2000." The resonant listener tries on what it feels like to have this desire. You resonate with it. That doesn't mean you have to agree with it. Far from it. You might want something entirely different. But understanding—true resonance—comes first, long before resolution. Remember: *Resonance precedes resolution*. The acid test of this skill comes when emotions are in the air. When someone says he's angry, the resonant listener tries on what it feels like for this person to be angry. The power of this move has to be seen to be believed.

Heath Herber, president of The Herber Company, told us: "I would say that listening to the other person's emotions may be the most important thing I've learned in twenty years in business. What I do is tune in to what's underneath the other person's words. It might be doubt. It might be irritation or nervousness. Then I just name it matter-of-factly. I say something like 'It sounds like you have some doubt, and I can sure understand why you might.' I never try to talk them out of it. If I can name it, they start to talk themselves out of it. I caught onto this one time when I was trying to sell a major contract to a car dealer. Things were bogged down and I couldn't figure out why. I knew I had the numbers that made sense to him, but he was stalling around. I saw that he was distracted about something, so I named it: 'You seem distracted, Charlie.' He blinked and shifted gears. 'Yeah, I guess I am. My daughter's getting married Saturday, and I'm having a lot of feelings about it.' It turned out our daughters were about the same age, but neither one of us until that moment even knew we had kids. Five minutes later I had a signed contract and a new friend."

LISTENING FOR MUTUAL CREATIVITY

The third stage of learning to listen comes when two people have done enough of stages one and two to develop an alliance. With the goodwill developed by stages one and two, they begin to listen to each other in a way that sparks the creativity of each to heights they could not have reached on their own. This deep listening—listening to inspire mutual creativity—is responsible for many breakthroughs in the world. Listening for mutual creativity is rooted in two questions: What do you most want? and How can I help you get what you most want? To listen in total support of other people—to be for their goals and aspirations in your own body, mind, and spirit—may well be the greatest gift you can give your fellow human beings.

Susan Snowe, one of the most effective corporate consultants we've met, gave us a great example of this deeper type of listening: "Once I was feeling stuck in my career. I scheduled a session with another consultant to help get me moving. After hearing my story, he asked me two questions over and over. The questions were 'What do you really want?' and 'Is that what you really want?' He gave me no information or advice—just those two questions. After about the third go-around, I realized that I wanted to start my own company. I'd been working for someone else for twenty years; now it was time for me to work for me. To this day I can feel the shift in my body that happened when I realized what I really wanted. It was as if all the stress and tension dropped away and rechanneled itself into energy."

GIVING AND RECEIVING HONEST FEEDBACK

One of the mystics interviewed for this book, Donna Kindl, was at one time head of human resources at Clorox. After a meeting she was taken aside by another woman executive: "The woman told me in harsh, nonsupportive language that I was arrogant and a terrible listener. At first, I was shocked, but as she continued talking I wanted to get down on my knees and express my gratitude. No one—not even my manager—had ever given me feedback like this. Even if it was exaggerated or colored by her personality, she was giving the gift of a lifetime by describing in excruciating detail how I came across. When she finished I expressed my thanks. She was so touched by my response that she took me under her wing and mentored me for the next few years."

We all need people
who will give us feedback.
That's how we improve.
If all my bridge coach ever told me
was that I was 'satisfactory,'
I would have no hope of ever getting better.

—BILL GATES,
FOUNDER, MICROSOFT

For many people the most difficult thing in communication is getting and giving honest feedback. Yet it is the most valuable commodity in the world. Many of the mystics we interviewed can give and receive feedback, even the brutally honest kind, in approximately the same tone of voice as they would give and hear the time of day. Their commitment to getting accurate data is higher than their commitment to being right.

> *People say I don't take criticism very well,*
> *but I say what the hell do they know?*
>
> —Attributed to Groucho Marx

BUILDING A CORPORATE CULTURE OF INTEGRITY

One of the authors has worked as a consultant for two companies with vastly different corporate cultures. Kate: "In one situation I was brought in because the senior management team was involved in major conflict between each other. All the people were veteran executives with one of these two companies, and all were imbued with a strong sense of the values and culture of their respective companies. The people from one company were accustomed to talking openly about their differences in meetings. Ideas were attacked, people were sometimes embarrassed, and the tone was often confrontational. However, these people were comfortable with this style, because to them it seemed up-front and honest. They felt they could trust each other because they knew where they stood.

To the veterans of the other company, this open style of communication seemed disrespectful and at worst, barbaric. They had grown up in a culture where you came into a meeting having worked out the issues one-to-one before the meeting so that there would be no surprises or hurt feelings. Meetings were to present "done deals," never places to flush out issues. You were expected to keep any contrary feelings to yourself and work them out one-to-one later.

The other company veterans saw this style as intensely political, leading to backroom deals and roundabout decision making. They felt they couldn't trust people to tell the truth in the meetings, so they never knew where anyone stood. The groups polarized: The slick Politicians versus the noisy Barbarians."

A look at the growth rates of both companies seems to favor the Barbarians, who have built a very successful company partly by placing a high value on telling the truth. In their case, integrity isn't a nicely framed value statement on the boardroom wall; it's a living, breathing way of working. The bottom line says that it pays off.

6

MANAGING PROJECTS

Life is either a daring adventure, or nothing.

—Helen Keller

Business success often depends on the art and science of course-correction. No one can predict when the next communication breakdown will occur or the next turf battle will erupt. Instead of a crystal ball, Corporate Mystics have an attitude that works wonders: They not only expect the unexpected but savor it.

We have often asked MBAs and others what was missing from their formal education—What did you have to learn "the hard way"? Frequently they have told us that their professors led them to believe that the course of business would be smooth, given careful planning and well-thought-out procedures. Breakdowns were regarded as symptoms, something to be avoided. In retrospect, however, they wish they had been told the opposite: Even with good planning and procedures, breakdowns are the normal and natural state of affairs. That's just the way it goes, and the businessperson who realizes this is in a much stronger position to deal with the vicissitudes of the day.

We begin with the worst-and best-case scenario.

HANDLING BIG WINS AND BIG LOSSES

Mystics learn to pay close attention just after a big success or a big loss. In both situations we are wide open and vulnerable, beyond our usual boundaries. These times are ripe for messing up.

Gay recalls a profound realization at the circus as a child: "A circus set up shop in a field near my house, and I got a job for a dime a day feeding the animals. This was back in the days when dimes were actually made of silver, so I thought I was getting the deal of a lifetime. One thing I noticed was that the elephants were tethered to a tiny peg that the trainer stuck in the ground. I could pull the peg out with two fingers, so I wondered to the trainer why the elephant didn't pull it out. He told me that the trick was to use a bigger peg when the elephant is little. The elephant cannot in the beginning budge the peg, so that it eventually stops trying to pull it out of the ground. The animal grows up with a clear sense of limitation. After a while, the elephant just knows it can't budge the peg, so you can tether several tons of elephant to a peg that a child could pull out of the ground. Most of us have some kind of limitation in our minds that we take as real. We don't realize that it is simply made up."

One of the key moves of life is to notice where we've got ourselves pegged to the ground. We need to look at our limitations and ask ourselves: If this peg weren't there, what would we do? What would we create? This is where the creativity comes from to start up a project or a company.

A big problem emerges right after you have pulled your peg out. Suddenly you're free, but you're also in the zone of the unknown. This is what often happens just after a big success. You've soared to a new level of power in your world and you may not yet have an internal structure to handle this new power. Rock stars are notorious for flaming out in their twenties; Alexander the Great had done all his conquering by the time of his death in his early thirties.

Just after a big success is a time to slow down a little, take a breath, re-center yourself. Do the same in times of loss. Just after a loss is a vulnerable time; there is a strong tendency in most of us to blame ourselves or others at times like that. When a loss has occurred it is very important to feel all of your feelings about it—anger, sadness, fear—then re-center yourself and ask: What most needs to be done right now?

The same wisdom applies to times of big loss. You are in the zone of the unknown, with pain instead of exhilaration in your body. There is a strong tendency to go into a blaming rather than a learning mode. You think: It's my fault, it's their fault, it's the world's fault. That way of thinking is normal, natural, and habitual. Human beings have been doing it that way for years. So don't beat up on yourself for dropping into that mode from time to time. As quickly as possible, though, shift to a learning mode. The questions then become: What can I learn from this? What revisioning is needed? What course corrections?

What most needs to be done right now?

GETTING THE RESPONSIBILITY FORMULA RIGHT

Most successful people are in the habit of taking more than 100 percent of the responsibility in work situations and life in general. This is a key trait, and you might not be where you are without it. So we're not suggesting you become less responsible, but you do need to be vigilant to make sure you're inspiring other people to be 100 percent responsible. In a situation involving two people, there is 200 percent responsibility to be divided up. With three people there is 300 percent. Responsibility goes up in multiples of 100 percent. The more people who are playing, the more important it becomes to have everyone taking their hundred.

Toward the top of companies most people are more-than-a-hundred-percent types. Down the line you get less-than-a-hundred types. For Corporate Mystics, the problem usually is learning to notice when they're operating in the more-than-a-hundred mode. How can you tell? The most reliable indicator is often what is going on in your body.

A budding mystic told us this story a few months after we had conducted a training in her company: "Until the training day when you explained how responsibility worked, I had no idea why I went home from work sometimes with crushing headaches. After the training I started tracking when I was taking responsibility that actually belonged to someone else. The headaches were coming from anger I was storing up about taking too much responsibility. I was angry at other people for not doing their share, and I was angry at myself for not knowing how to motivate them to do so. As I began to set myself the task of giving people room to be 100 percent responsible, I woke up one day and realized I hadn't had a headache in over a month. That to me is close to being a miracle."

How do you motivate others to do their 100 percent? Delegation is the usual answer, and there is no question that it's a crucial skill for outstanding leaders—one that you have to practice until it's second nature. But delegation, important as it is, is not the fundamental issue. It boils down to your basic position in life: Do you feel that people are fundamentally equal? Do you genuinely feel that people are capable of operating at the 100 percent level?

Michelangelo is said to have looked at a raw block of marble and seen the statue of David in it. Do we see ourselves, and other people, as masterpieces waiting to happen?

> *I like to be challenged through questions and
> thought provoking discussions, not necessarily directed.
> I perform better in that kind of environment,
> so I strive to challenge people, their intellectual side
> and their competitive spirit.*
>
> —ANNETTE CLAYTON,
> CEO, SCHNEIDER ELECTRIC NORTH AMERICA

REAL POWER

Jerry Jones, a Portland developer and first-class Corporate Mystic, told us: "Some of the best deals I ever made were ones I chose not to make. Earlier in my career I would often beat things to death with energy, trying to make things happen that I should have probably left alone in the first place. As I've matured spiritually and in business, I've learned to listen to the flow. If something is taking a tremendous amount of energy—if it hurts to do it—it may be something you shouldn't be doing. I might compare it to sailing. If you watch the winds carefully you can take advantage of the way they're blowing. Sometimes it's fun to beat into the wind, but over the long haul it eats up too much energy.

"On an airplane flight a while back, I was sitting next to Philip Knight, head of Nike Corporation. Behind us was a fellow who was a middle management type. He spent the flight making phone calls, barking orders, generating a tremendous amount of energy and noise. It was as if he was trying to get people to see how important he was. Meanwhile Phil, a billionaire whose company provides jobs for thousands of people, spent his time thinking, reading, napping. There was a tangible aura of serenity around him. It made me realize how much energy gets wasted in business by ego and displays of false power. By contrast, real power comes from your inner contact with yourself and the universe."

As a practical step in this direction, Jerry does two things that all Corporate Mystics might consider. He spends the first hour of his business day in meditation. With his contact with his inner self and the universe refreshed, he then moves into action. His second edge is to spend each Thursday in complete silence. He will send faxes and such, but he does not have any conversations with people. Both he and his staff have found that this "time-out" is extremely productive. They appreciate a day without his verbal input because it gives them a chance to catch up on assignments from earlier in the week. Once, during a busy spell, he thought he would cut out the Silent Thursday for the sake of the staff. However, they begged him to continue because they were so impressed with the value of it for his well-being and creativity.

RETAINING HIGH-POTENTIAL EMPLOYEES

One of the challenges in corporate life is keeping good people. Paradoxically, as corporations mature they often have a harder time retaining creative people. Bureaucracy grows, rules rigidify, communication must pass through more and more levels. Many of the creative people we have met in corporate environments privately expressed their deep frustration with the strictures of their rule-bound workplaces. When Kate was vice-president for human resources at KLA Instruments, she used intuition, listening, truth telling, and good, old-fashioned creativity to keep a valuable employee: "Mark was an engineering vice-president, a creative guy who had probably brought in $300 million with his designs. I didn't know him well, nor did I see him very often because he worked in a different building. But one morning I kept having uncomfortable thoughts about him tugging at me. Following my intuition, I drove my car over to his building and knocked on his door. I found him staring off into space, confused and unhappy. I sat down and asked him what was going on. After a few minutes of evading the issue, he finally spilled it out. He had just received an offer from another company and was thinking about leaving his job with us.

"I was stunned because he seemed so irreplaceable and so much a part of our culture. I've learned, though, that it never works to 'buy people' because people don't work for money. So I pulled out all my listening skills and drew out of him what the problem was. It took a couple of hours to get the whole story. It turned out that he hated his commute and the administrative aspects of his job, which kept him away from his two children and his wife, who was pregnant with a third child. The commute was a real sticking point; it took him an hour and a half if he came during rush hour and an hour if he came early and stayed late. The other company was five minutes from his house, which made it look very attractive in spite of his love for his work with us.

"I cleared my calendar and we spent a day and a half designing his perfect job. At first it was tough, because none of the things he thought of as a perfect job were things he could visualize ever happening at KLA. Eventually we arrived at a creative solution which met all of his needs and those of the company. We rented a small suite for him in an office building down the street from his house, and set it up so that he only had to come into the main office twice a week for major meetings. We brought in a pure management person who took over the administrative aspect of Mark's job, freeing him up to put his attention on his first love, designing new technology. When I left a year later, he was still happy with the arrangement."

USING INTUITION TO AVOID A COSTLY MISTAKE

A Corporate Mystic and CEO of a Silicon Valley firm tells how intuition came through for him in an acquisitions deal: "The chairman of the board was very hot to acquire a company back east that had designed a new technology that he thought would fit our company's long-range goals. I knew nothing about the company and did not have much of a feel for the technology, either, but as I thought about it I kept having the urge to talk to one of our vice-presidents about it. This was an unusual thought, because she normally would not be involved in any project of this nature. Nevertheless I followed my intuition and met with her. We mutually decided to have her fly east the next day to meet with the principals of the company. She returned after the meeting with a nagging feeling that there was something wrong, but she couldn't put her finger on it. She had liked the people but there was something 'funny' about the business. We decided to spend more time and money investigating the company, only to find that there were major problems with their approach to the technology. Essentially, there was no market in the way they had approached it. Listening to my gut ended up saving the company millions of dollars, even though following my intuition meant bucking the desires of the board chairman. In the long run, though, he came to appreciate the choice we made, especially when he saw the waste that would have occurred."

HANDLING COMPLAINERS AND LOW PRODUCERS

When people are not producing, it is usually because they are out of integrity with themselves. They are not doing what they really want to be doing. The post office is full of people who want to be writers, while writers often dream of a simple job like sorting mail. Your task, if you're the kindhearted sort, is to talk with these people and ask them, "What do you want to be doing?" If you can help them find a way to do it, great. If not, get them out the door as soon as possible. The post office can't do this, but you probably can.

Complainers complain because they are out of integrity, too, but their integrity breaches go deeper. They are out of integrity with themselves first and foremost, but they are usually out of integrity with the organization, too. Sometimes complaints are valid, but people who complain a lot are usually out of integrity and don't want to admit it. Your loudest complainer about office fairness will reliably turn out to be your big paper-clip thief. A mystic manager recalls: "The president hired in a superstar from another company who started complaining practically the moment he arrived. After listening for a while, most of us tuned it out and assumed it was a character problem. One night I got the proof. I was working late, with the holidays approaching, and I saw our man come into his office with his wife. 'That's unusual,' I thought. During the several hours they were there I had to make numerous trips past his office. Every time I passed they were talking to their relatives! They had come to the office to make their holiday calls! Not long after this, our superstar disappeared from the scene."

HOW TO HANDLE AN OFFICE AFFAIR

Sexual affairs can be a difficult problem for all concerned. A Corporate Mystic we know used the integrity tools outlined earlier to clear up an awkward situation that was hindering a major project.

"I was a vice-president at the time, and the company was about to launch a major new product. Everybody was tense and working eighty to ninety hours a week, so when the rumor mill started grinding it sent tremors through the whole operation. The rumor was that a general manager who reported to me was having an affair with a woman who reported to him. Both were married. At first I was stumped; nobody had told me how to deal with this sort of thing in my MBA school, and I had never confronted it before.

"As I sat down to mull over what to do, I realized I was conflicted in my values. I didn't see myself as the arbiter of somebody else's ethics, but on the other hand I knew all about sexual harassment suits, too. I mainly was concerned that the lying and covering up would throw everything off kilter at a critical time in the company's evolution. I decided to take action. I checked out the source, to understand if there were any documentable facts. There were. So

I went to see the man himself. In his office I told him that I was hearing the rumor. I told him that I didn't know or need to know if it was true. I explained everything that had gone through my mind and everything I'd heard. I told him what I saw as the consequences if the rumor were true, both for him and for the company. Then I explained the legal risks as well as I could. He didn't say much during the meeting. He looked down a lot as I was talking to him, showing body language that made him look guilty.

"Two days later I heard that the woman in question had been transferred to a different position, with mutual satisfaction all around. The rumor mill died down, and within a year both people had been promoted. The project went off successfully, giving me all the proof I needed that telling the truth had healed the situation."

ENDING TURF BATTLES

One of the main drainers of corporate energy is the turf war. One of the mystics we interviewed for this book put it plainly: "If turf battles were not going on in most American corporations, there would be no trade deficit with Japan. The Japanese have figured out a way to get by without this kind of junior-high-school stuff. Maybe their way is too hierarchical for American tastes, but we've got to figure some way before there's no way."

You've seen it a hundred times. Manager X squabbles with Manager Y over who would do the best job on a project. Or Manager Z won't share his data with Manager A. The message is: This is my turf and you can't come in here. Our monkey cousins do it very directly. Get on their turf and they spit at you or toss something even more unpleasant at you. Anyone who has spent time in organizations will have a healthy respect for the power of this monkey business to limit productivity. One longtime corporate officer told us that ceiling tiles were a turf benchmark in her company. People actually counted their ceiling tiles to determine the exact square footage of their offices.

As consultants, we often are called in when turf problems have gotten out of hand. We have found that most turf wars could have been avoided by ten minutes of authentic, heartfelt communication. Often, when everything resolves, it is because the main parties put together that few minutes of plain talking that could have been there in the beginning.

Turf battles usually backfire to hurt the people who started them. We have seen this happen so often that it has given us faith that there is a type of justice or karma at work in the world. Here is a typical example: A new marketing vice-president (we'll call him Mark) was hired and seemed to be doing a good job at first. After a couple of months he developed a personal animosity toward one of the engineering managers and began blaming all sorts of problems on him. After much politicking on Mark's part, the engineering manager stepped back from an active management role. It looked at first as though Mark had won, but a very different outcome soon unfolded. The CEO had become so disenchanted with Mark's blame-oriented behavior that he was the next to go.

In a turf war, it becomes more important to be right than to do a good job with the project at hand. In Mark's case, his driving need to be right cost him the ability to see the bigger picture, only to get a rude awakening just as he was celebrating his victory over the other guy.

We were called in to help end a turf war that had cost a small fortune in time, energy, and money. It happened in one of America's largest consumer-products companies, and it could have been avoided by that ten minutes of clear communication we mentioned earlier: "During a vision retreat off-site, the whole engineering staff got very turned on about setting a new product direction. As the high of this new direction buzzed through the room, they sent for the marketing vice-president, Perry, to get him as fired up as they were. He had been in a much duller meeting and came in cold, with no preparation as to what the engineers had been envisioning. He became flustered and went into overwhelm. He proclaimed that it was his job to come up with new product directions. Jack, head of the engineering team, tried to explain that they were just excitedly brainstorming and wanted to fill him in. Perry wasn't having any of it and stormed out.

"Jack and Perry were as different as two people in the high-tech world can get. Jack was an honest, technical sort without a shred of political savvy. He described himself as a 'political boob.' The other man, Perry, was a very skilled corporate politician, a honey-voiced salesman in an Armani suit. After the meeting they got into a turf battle that lasted two years. By the time we were brought in, the conflict had spread through three levels of management. We set a deadline, to work two days and into the second night if we had to, but nobody was going to leave until it got sorted out. As the deadline approached on the second evening, they finally made a breakthrough. They saw that there had been a massive misperception of each other's intentions in the original situation two years before. They went back to that moment and talked about their fears and how these fears had colored their perceptions of the events. There was a major meltdown of tension in the room as these two 'worthy opponents' accepted each other."

What to do about turf battles? First, see them clearly for what they are: one primate, living in fear, trying to keep another primate from booting him out of the leadership position. Once you see that it is "gorilla warfare," you are in a much stronger position. You've called the game for what it actually is. The next thing to do is to look inside yourself. Are you participating in any turf-protecting dramas? Naturally, it is harder to see them in yourself than in others. But take a hard look at yourself first.

Next you have to choose your way out of the game. You do this by making a decision not to participate in or support turf bathes. You find yourself looking up at those ceiling tiles, and instead of counting them again, you take a deep breath and bring yourself back to the real issue: your resonance with your inner self and your creative contribution to the enterprise at hand.

HOW TO KEEP MEETINGS FROM BEING BORING

In our role as consultants, we are frequently asked to facilitate meetings. We have noticed that meetings often do not produce results because not everyone is taking total responsibility for the meeting's success. Often, in fact, the only people engaged are the person who called the meeting and the people who oppose that person or the issue. We evolved a strategy to get total involvement, and it really works.

> *Try never to be the smartest person in the room.*
> *And if you are, I suggest you invite smarter people....*
> *or find a different room.*
>
> —Michael Dell,
> CEO and Chairman, Dell Technologies

We put a ten-point rating scale on the board, with ten being "totally involved" and one being "bored to death." Every fifteen minutes we ask people to rate themselves and to do what's necessary to get to ten. Most people are willing to admit their lack of interest, but they often blame this on the team, the leader, or the content of the meeting. When they begin to take responsibility—when they see that it is their own boredom that is making the meeting boring—magic begins to occur. The team members begin to see what produces boredom and what produces involvement. They shift toward feeling responsible for producing involvement, and that is sometimes the only shift that needs to be made.

TURNING ADVERSE SITUATIONS INTO BREAKTHROUGHS

What makes a breakdown happen is very simple. You can see it in the corner shoe-repair shop and you can see it at GM or IBM. What happens first is that some event occurs. The event itself could be as small as a delivery not being made or as large as a stock market crash. The event itself does not cause a breakdown. It is the people-reaction to the event that causes the problem.

> *The winners of tomorrow will deal proactively*
> *with chaos, will look at the chaos per se*
> *as the source of market advantage,*
> *not as a problem to be gotten around.*
>
> —Tom Peters

The breakdown is caused by diverting attention into one unproductive line of inquiry: Whose fault is this? Sometimes a scapegoat is found: It's his fault or her fault. Other times the fault is located outside: It's the world's fault. Occasionally you will get lucky, pinpoint a scapegoat, and fire the person. But it's hard to fire the world. The night before committing suicide, Hitler dictated his last will and testament, disavowing any responsibility for the war and blaming it on the Jews. Some people just never seem to get the message.

There is only one productive line of inquiry in a crisis: What can we learn? What needs to be done? Shifting focus to learning and doing what needs to be done always changes a breakdown to a breakthrough.

7

CREATING WEALTH

All the Corporate Mystics we interviewed for this book agreed on one thing: Wealth begins in the human mind. We focused many of our interviews on men and women who had earned their wealth rather than inheriting it. We found that their belief systems about wealth were surprisingly uniform. They had all made conscious decisions to generate abundance for themselves and others. The tools they used were different. Some tapped into the robust stream of wisdom represented by Napoleon Hill, George Classon, and other writers on prosperity and success. Some used techniques of their own devising, learning their prosperity lessons in that most rigorous of business schools: Hard-Knox.

In this chapter we will summarize every key principle we discovered in our conversations with Corporate Mystics. These are all tools real people have used successfully; we present them for your experimentation. We have also used them in our own successful quest for financial independence. May they work for you as well as they have worked for us.

You may be disappointed if you fail,
but you will be doomed if you don't try.

—Beverly Sills

ENLIGHTENED PERSEVERANCE

The corporate woods are full of what the music business calls one-hit wonders. These are people who have a burst of success, then quickly flame out, mess up, or fade away. If you want to be abundant in money, love, or anything else, you have to show up consistently. Persistence will win out over creativity and talent just about every time. Was John Belushi a better comedian than Jay Leno? Doesn't matter much now, does it?

> *Stay the course. Behaviors change slowly. Time is often the most important investment you can make. It will take more than one try to make an impact, and it will take more than one success to make a difference.*
>
> —JANET MOUNTAIN,
> DIRECTOR, MICHAEL AND SUSAN DELL FOUNDATION

Gay had lunch with a radiant man of seventy in his mountaintop retreat. This man, a millionaire many times over, had walked from Germany to the coast of France as a teenager to stay a step ahead of the Nazis. He got on a boat and came to America, where he knew no one and did not speak the language. By the end of his thirties he had a wife and a family and had built a thousand houses. Hot with success, he built up a $5 million fortune and sat back to live the good life. Then came an economic downturn. Not only did he go bankrupt, but he was stuck with a vast amount of lumber. Within fifteen years he had gone from penniless to millionaire to bankrupt. Did it bother him? "Hell, yes, it bothered me! But you have to get back up and go again. Every minute you spend thinking about the way it used to be or the way it ought to be is a minute you haven't been thinking about the way I could make it be. I had a couple of things going for me, though. The main one was that once you've walked five hundred miles in the winter to get away from Nazis, dealing with a bunch of angry bankers is like a picnic. The other advantage I had is persistence. I had it when I was a kid and I've got it right this minute. I know if I just keep getting up in the morning and looking for some contribution to make, I'm going to have a good day."

> *Eighty percent of success is just showing up.*
>
> —WOODY ALLEN

This attitude served him well. The Vietnam War heated up as he was trying to unload his extra lumber, and he became one of the primary suppliers of wood products to the war. Soon he was back in the millionaire ranks and hasn't looked back.

If you match creativity and talent with some persistence, you have a powerful combination. Corporate Mystics know that the secret to showing up consistently is to reframe adversity into challenge. If you consider it a setback when you get dumped off the horse, you don't have a very good time learning to ride. If you see it as part of the process, a necessary and fundamental aspect of riding, you have a context for adversity that allows you to keep your eyes on the goal.

> *Nothing in the world can take the place of persistence:*
> *Talent will not; nothing is more common than*
> *unsuccessful men with great talent. Genius will not:*
> *unrewarded genius is almost a proverb. Education*
> *will not: the world is full of educated derelicts.*
> *Persistence and determination alone are omnipotent.*
>
> —CALVIN COOLIDGE

The difference between successful people and leaders who create breakthrough success is that these people say no to almost everything. Numerous founders of highly successful companies, including Steve Jobs, Michael Dell, Bill Gates, and Warren Buffett have attributed their success to focus. Many people have long to-do lists and work on becoming more productive, when in fact, having a not-do list is more important if you want to do great things.

> *It's easy to decide what you're going to do.*
> *The hard thing is deciding*
> *what you're not going to do.*
>
> —Michael Dell,
> CEO and Chairman, Dell Technologies

HAVING WHAT YOU WANT

The first secret to wealth: Wealth is having what you want. The second secret: Wealth is enjoying what you have. You will hear compelling arguments against both of these ideas. Just about everybody will have a good reason why you shouldn't have what you want. The world is full of people who will argue forcefully for mediocrity and settling for less. Don't listen to them. Others will have great reasons why you shouldn't enjoy what you have. There is so much suffering in the world that many people think that's the way it's supposed to be. Don't listen to them, either. It is perfectly acceptable to have what you want and enjoy what you have. From this place it is possible to facilitate others in having what they want and enjoying what they have. That's where the big fun is to be had in life. A wise person once said that a life of total leisure is the hardest career to pursue. Human beings are not built for unrestricted leisure. Contribution is the driving force of the truly successful person. To the Corporate Mystics we interviewed for the book, the desire for contribution to others' lives was a paramount motivation.

Along the way, why not have what you want and enjoy what you have?

One of the authors' friends decided she wanted to go to medical school. "You can't," said everyone from her mother to the dean of the local medical school, "you're forty-four years old!" She applied to several schools and was turned down at all of them. Finally, she applied to a university in Holland. They accepted her. "See you in three months," they said, "and by the way, all the lectures are in Dutch. Be sure you are fluent when you get here." At the time she spoke not a word of Dutch, but three months later she was fluent. She's now a practicing physician in her early fifties, having what she wants.

Gay was resting on a park bench in Paris, sipping a cup of coffee and feeding the birds. "A woman in her late sixties sat down beside me and we struck up a conversation. She mentioned she had just arrived from Portugal. Oh, I asked, how did you, make the journey?

" 'I walked,' she said, and told me that she had decided when she retired at sixty-two to walk around the world, starting from Arizona. Friends and family mounted a fierce campaign to talk her out of it, but she wasn't listening. First she walked to California, then she changed her mind and went the other direction. She was on her eleventh pair of sneakers when I met her. Noticing her wedding ring, I asked her where her husband was. Back in Arizona, she said. 'I asked him to come, but he didn't want to. Said he'd rather stay home and watch TV.' But she hadn't let that stop her."

As consultants, we have had the opportunity to talk to many people who have done the business equivalent of going off for a walk around the world. One man left a corporate job he found stultifying to found his own company. He went from a plush office with a view of the Chicago Loop to a little facility in an industrial park on the outskirts of town. "But, at least, it was my name on the door. There was no one responsible for me but me, myself, and I." After two years his company failed. "But, you know what? I felt happier even dealing with the failure than I had in the previous five years with the other company." Two years after that failure, though, he had bounced back and was one of the industry leaders.

We have talked to fifty people or more who have taken the plunge and started their own companies. Of those fifty, only twenty or so have been successful. But we cannot think of one who has regretted the move. Something good has come out of it, even though it often did not fit the picture they originally had.

ENJOYING WHAT YOU HAVE

Once you have what you want you will be faced with the problem of enjoying it all in a world filled with shame and scarcity. Don't buy into this, either. Go ahead: Have what you want. You'll know if it's something you really want if you're willing to walk around the world for it. But then, once you've got it, you still have the challenge of enjoying what you've got.

A Corporate Mystic of our acquaintance wrangled an invitation to visit a man worth $100 million. The man's jaw muscles clenched constantly as he described his desperate desire to get to billionaire status. He chain-smoked and carped at his wife throughout the discussion, which was carried out in his underground bunker/fallout shelter, four stories beneath where his dream house glittered in the afternoon sun. He seldom left the bunker to go up the elevator to the dream house. He said the natural beauty tended to interfere with the concentration he needed to work. Although all signs said he had it made, he did not have what he wanted and he was not enjoying what he had.

Mystics realize that satisfaction and enjoyment are completely within their control, so they start there. They work on enjoying what they have, exactly as it is now.

There are two things to aim at in life;
first, to get what you want; and after that, to enjoy it.
Only the wisest of mankind achieve the second.

—LOGAN PEARSALL SMITH

THE FUNDAMENTAL LAW OF CREATING WEALTH

The first law of creating wealth is this: You can choose what you think. You can choose any goal you want, and you can make up any financial rule you choose to live by, as long as it does not interfere with any fundamental rules of how the universe works. There is no limit to what you can think up. To make it live in the material world, you have to support it with action, but the key moment is taking responsibility for thinking it up the way you want it. If you really understand the significance of this law, you are in a position to create genuine miracles for yourself and for your organization.

All wealth comes from the human mind. In Zurich it may be measured in gold or by blips on a computer screen. On a remote South Pacific island it may be measured in cowrie shells. But always and everywhere it is based on pure agreement, constructed by the creative power of the human mind.

The good news is that we all carry that same creative power within us. If you understand the nature of your own consciousness, you will see how wealth is generated.

The human mind has evolved to the point that we now can consciously perceive ourselves as connected to the infinite. Many of us do not, of course, choose to celebrate this connection or use it to make us happy. But we have the potential, all the same, of opening up to a seamless relationship with all creation.

> *We are what we think.*
> *All that we are arises with our thoughts.*
> *With our thoughts we make our world.*
>
> —THE BUDDHA

As soon as we embrace our connection with the infinite, we can see that we are connected to the source of creativity. The same creative force that makes oak trees, dolphins, and rainbows also makes us. An acorn is something that was created out of nothingness, and it has the seeds of creation hidden in potential within it. It is at once created and creator.

We are a microcosm of the whole universe. We carry creator and created within us.

You have the power to create something from nothing. You can think up any reality you want. As long as it does not conflict with any laws of the universe, it can manifest, providing you support it with whatever actions are required. In other words, you can make up the rules, as long as your rules don't conflict with the other rules. The thought "I enjoy complete abundance of love and money" does not conflict with any laws of the universe. Put your attention on it, support it with action, and it will come into being. If you make up a rule that says "I can steal without getting caught," you probably won't succeed because it conflicts with other rules in the world. The thought "By flapping my arms I can fly like an eagle" conflicts with a current law of the universe. You can think it all day long and it won't become reality. If you want to argue this point, send us a picture first and we'll get in touch.

Nobody would be harmed by a new rule in the universe that says "I am abundant in love and money." If you are ready and willing to be abundant in love and money, step into the creator role: Go ahead and choose it now.

Say the words and get the body-feeling: "I am ready and willing to be abundant in love and money."

Go one step further. Put it in the present tense.

"I am abundant in love and money." Feel it in your body as a right-now reality.

You can bring into creation anything you want, as long as it's in harmony with the fundamental way the universe works. Some thoughts that have a great deal of power are:

> "My income is always much larger than my expenses."
> "Every dollar I spend comes back to me multiplied."
> "I effortlessly have plenty of money to do everything I want to do."
> "The more people I make prosperous, the more prosperous I become."

There is no limit to what you can think up.

Money doesn't buy happiness,
but that's not why so many people are poor.

—LAURENCE PETER

The greatest discovery of my generation is that
a human being can alter his life
by altering his attitudes of mind.

—WILLIAM JAMES

HOW TO CREATE A MIND-SET OF PROSPERITY IN YOUR ORGANIZATION

You carry your abundance or lack of abundance with you night and day. It is not in your portfolio or bank account. There are many, many people with large amounts of money who are stingy, unpleasant, greedy, and unhappy. There are just as many living in a virtual garden of love who do not open to it or appreciate it. So abundance of love and money begins in our consciousness. We have charge of it. We can say: I consciously choose abundance of love and money in my life.

You can make this choice individually with great rewards, but a more powerful set of possibilities emerges when you do this as a group or as an entire company. We have been in meetings in which an entire executive team opened up to choosing abundance for themselves as individuals and for the company at large. When the individuals coalesced into a team, the shift in consciousness could be felt throughout the room. The late Andrew Carnegie taught that if you could get five people into harmony around a goal, you could generate miracles. It worked for him; he funded fourteen hundred libraries around the world through his philanthropy, with change left over for a couple of universities.

The benefit of abundance consciousness is you can take it wherever you go in the world. If you know that your abundance begins in your mind, you create love and money anywhere. If you do not know this, you can sit in the middle of a pile of money in a garden of love and not know how to access either one.

It all begins in your consciousness. And you invoke it by choosing.

Right now, make the choice.

I choose complete abundance in love and money.

Or not. It is completely your own choice.

If you want abundance, choose it carefully and calmly. Bring it into being by thinking and feeling this idea: *I choose complete abundance in love and money.*

TURNING AROUND NEGATIVE FINANCIAL ATTITUDES

Once you invoke abundance in your life, you will be able to see more clearly where you are operating from limiting beliefs about yourself or about the world. Our most limiting beliefs will not even be revealed until after we have made a commitment to abundance. Right after you choose abundance you may think, "These ideas will never work for me." This is the limiting thought that has been released into the light by the power of your commitment to abundance. Any negative thoughts that surface as you consider these ideas can be regarded as old limits put in your mind by you or someone else. Don't make them right or wrong; just let them move on through.

There is a specific technology that is helpful when those limiting thoughts bubble up: Use a positive thought to replace the old limiting concept. Let's say you find yourself thinking: "I always lose money in the stock market." You wouldn't have a limiting thought like that unless you or someone you identify with had been wounded and infected with scarcity. When you uncover a wound, use the healing power of your own thoughts to soothe it. Think "All my investments are profitable." You might surface a limiting thought like "I could never be financially secure." Apply a more positive thought: Think "I have complete financial abundance." One good way to apply a positive thought is to drop it into your thought-stream as soon as you notice a limiting thought go by.

Applying a positive thought takes your negativity out of the situation. Perhaps your stock market investments will improve or perhaps you'll take all your money out of the stock market. Either way you win. But at least you will not be carrying around that blotch of negativity with you.

Once you have begun identifying your own negativity about money, look around you at the key people in your life. See if they are carrying negative attitudes. The reason this is important is that alignment with two or three key people in your life can produce abundance much more quickly. If you are linked to a life partner who has scarcity programming they won't confront, it makes your journey to abundance much more difficult. Sit down and talk it out. Find out if your friends and family would join you in a mutual quest for abundance.

Definitely find out where your main business partners stand on this issue. Do they understand, believe, and practice the principle that we generate wealth first in our own minds? If they do, great! If not, you need to help tune them up or you will be dragged down by them.

CLEAN UP YOUR UNFINISHED FINANCIAL BUSINESS

A powerful key to creating abundance is to start taking care of any unfinished business in your money life. Start with two main categories: *Money I Owe* and *Money I Am Owed*. Take out a sheet of paper right now and put these two categories on it. List anything you can think of, going back as far as you can.

Gay received the following letter from a woman who had taken his course for consultants: "I committed to complete several pieces of unfinished business in the area of money at our March meeting. The unfinished business included relatively trivial items like $15 I owed someone, up to significant items like $23,000 someone owed me and the unresolved issue of ownership of a house. Within ten days after the training I repaid all the monies I owed people, hired a lawyer to go after the $23,000, and flew to Hawaii to negotiate the agreements about the house. In April I had my first $15,000 month as a consultant, more than doubling any month I'd ever had in the past."

It is important to realize that you don't have to take care of all your unfinished business at once. All you have to do is start the process. You may owe $1,000 and have only $10. It doesn't matter. The important thing is to make a start. Send the $10 to the person or open an account with the intention of putting a dollar a day toward the debt. You'll be surprised at how quickly your actions will be rewarded with abundance.

LEADING WITH GRATITUDE

One of the most powerful tools for creating abundance is leading with gratitude. Here's how it works, as described by Gay: "In the mid-eighties I began confronting my limiting ideas about how prosperous I could be. Soon, I began having spontaneous thoughts of people with whom I had financial incompletions. Two of these were John and Bill, both of whom had loaned me money years before. They had disappeared from the screen of my life, and I had conveniently 'forgotten' about the debts.

"One thing I learned from Buckminster Fuller was to act on an idea within ten minutes of having it (I think he was talking about business ideas, not ones about showroom Ferraris or people to whom you're sexually attracted!). As soon as I realized why John and Bill were appearing in my mind, I started trying to find them. I found Bill with a couple of weeks' research and wrote him to tell him I wanted to pay him back. His circumstances had changed radically, such that he was now nearly destitute. He indicated that the money would mean a great deal to him. John was more difficult; to this day I have not located him. I put his money into circulation by dispersing it to various charities I thought he would approve of.

"My wife, Kathlyn, and I started to work systematically on discovering incompletions and taking care of them. They nearly always turned out to be in the area of things we needed to communicate to people. For example, Kathlyn and I both realized that we had never formally and completely thanked several members of our families who had helped us out financially when we were in graduate school. My mother had sold a piece of property worth about $10,000, and had split the proceeds with me and my brother. Kathlyn's parents had come through with a $2,500 loan while she was working on her doctorate. We wrote several detailed letters of appreciation and gratitude, and were richly rewarded by a tide of good feeling that rushed back our way.

"In addition to the good feeling, this process started us thinking about what we now call 'leading with gratitude.' Many of us are waiting for something good to happen, then we'll express some gratitude. Maybe. It is akin to a gardener saying to the garden, 'Give me some flowers and then I'll water you.' But we found a better way, which was to make the expression of gratitude an ongoing process. Focus on gratitude first: Lead with appreciation. Our practical step was to look for ways we could express gratitude to people in our lives. This, more than any other principle, began to turn our lives toward prosperity."

*A pat on the back,
though only a few vertebrae
removed from a kick in the pants,
is miles ahead in results.*

—BENNETT CERF,
CO-FOUNDER, RANDOM HOUSE

FACING YOUR
INTERNAL ENEMIES OF ABUNDANCE

In our consulting work, we have found several main barriers people face even at the very highest levels of corporate life. In fact, the more successful you become, the more likely you are to encounter them. Those who are not conscious of these barriers often trip over them or sabotage their success because of them.

The first is the fear of rising to your full measure of success because of unconscious loyalties to people in your past. Many of us grew up in families or went to schools where we felt guilty about outdoing others. We had to pretend to know less than we did, or we felt guilty that not everyone could win the prize we won. Later in life, when success strikes, we may not enjoy it fully because we still carry this guilt about outdoing someone else.

There is another version of this fear: By being fully successful we will leave someone else behind. The origins of this fear are usually in our family lives, in our guilt about abandoning someone less capable than ourselves. Perhaps it is a younger sibling or a retarded family member; there is often someone we have to leave behind, and it hurts to do so. Later that hurt haunts us so that we do not go into our full abundance for fear of: abandoning others. For example, both Gay and his brother, Mike, were the first members of their family to attend college. "Both of us felt mixed feelings of pride and guilt. We knew people in the family were proud of us, but we also felt guilty that we were doing things they never had a chance to do," recalls Gay. "I felt a strong need to reassure them, when I went home to visit, that I still loved them. I was sometimes hesitant to tell them about stimulating cultural events I attended, for fear that they would feel bad."

Unless you bring this fear to light, you run a risk as you grow in your career. The typical pattern is to commit an act of self-sabotage based on this fear. You have a big win, for example, then mess up in some way or get sick. Family scripts are powerful teachers, for better and for worse. Many successful people come from humble beginnings and have worked hard to transcend the family script. Yet at the same time they may carry unconscious fears that their success is somehow being disloyal to the family. We have worked with many such executives to help them acknowledge and release their unconscious loyalties to those in their past. As the burden of guilt is lifted, successful people find that they can love and appreciate the people in their past more easily.

IS YOUR SUCCESS A BURDEN?

A second internal barrier is the fear that our abundance might be a burden in some way. In today's ecologically sensitive environment, there is widespread concern that the creations of humankind place a burden on the earth's natural resources. There is a great deal of validity to this perception, and each person must face his or her obligation to the planet as part of each corporate decision. However, there is a more personal problem that successful people must face.

As consultants we have often worked with people who have grown up feeling they were burdens to their families. Sometimes this perception was based on realities such as poverty or illness. If you actually are a burden in some way to your parents, you may internalize and carry this feeling into adult life. More frequently, though, the burden was imaginary. Imaginary or real, the net result is often the same: Their success as adults is dampened by a concern that it is a burden to the world. One of our clients grew up in quite a wealthy family, but he was the last-born of five, the last two of whom were accidental pregnancies. Both grew up with a pervasive sense that their very existence was unwelcome, based largely on nonverbal messages they received. Our client didn't make this connection until later in his thirties, when he found that he was not moving as fast as he wanted on his career track. He was also motivated by his older brother's entry into a drug and alcohol rehabilitation program. As he confronted his unconscious fears, he found that he had perceived himself as a burden from the first moments of his awareness in life. When he cleared the issue up, he moved ahead quickly in his career and later went into the family business, which he had always resisted joining.

Related to this is a fear that our abundance might be taking from others. We may think: If I am fully abundant it will cause someone else to suffer lack. It is very rare for this to be the case, but many people suffer from this fear because of early programming. They were made to feel in their families that their existence took love and attention away from someone else.

With all of these barriers, the simple act of awareness takes their power away. Noting them and seeing which ones pertain to you is the most liberating step you can take.

DOING WHAT YOU LOVE

The happiest mystics we have met are those who are doing what they most love to do. Many of them ask this question on a regular basis: What do I love to do that adds real value to people's lives? Gay has based his whole career on this question: "I was sitting at home one evening when I was still in my twenties, thinking about what I really wanted to do with my life. I had recently heard a lecture by J. Krishnamurti in which he said that the sole purpose of education was to help you find out what you, with all your heart, most love to do. With this in mind, I asked myself what I most loved to do. Ten minutes of wondering later, I had come up with several ideas. One was that I loved to write. The act of putting words on paper delighted me. The second thing I loved to do was to sit around with interesting people discussing the most fundamental issues of living. Putting these two together, I dreamed up a career of writing about and consulting with people about the most important psychospiritual concerns human beings face. If I could do that, I thought, I would make full use of my talents while never feeling like I was working for a living.

"Next I found myself confronting my limited thinking: A loud, mocking voice in my head said, 'You could never make a living doing that! Who would pay for that?' At first, I took this voice seriously and felt a wave of despair course through me. Then I thought 'Wait a minute!' I recognized the mocking voice as belonging to my older brother. That was his voice and his attitude! He's an air-conditioning and heating contractor, so naturally he wouldn't think much of a career in applied metaphysics. I let go of the negative voice and took a deep breath. Next, an image of one of my Stanford professors flashed through my mind. It was a memory of my saying to him that I wanted to put the powerful learnings of psychology into forms that everyone could use. He sneered with utter derision, 'Surely you're not thinking of becoming one of those pop psychologists!' His tone made it sound like I was going to mass-market bubonic plague.

"I took a few more breaths and let that old painful image go. I realized that what I wanted to do was groundbreaking in my family tradition and my classical psychology background. There was not going to be much agreement there for my goals: I would have to manufacture my own agreement. Right then and there I made a deal between me and the universe that I would go for what I wanted, which was to make a living doing what I most love to do. And that's the way it's been."

PULLING THE PLUG ON DRAIN-RELATIONSHIPS

Unless you are very lucky, you have certain relationships that drain your energy. These relationships decrease your energy, your money supply, and your free time. Usually we put up with them for some other reason, perhaps because they involve family or friends.

These relationships can be changed radically if you are courageous enough to take action. For those relationships where you are not obligated by blood ties or binding legal contracts, we recommend a process we call high-firing. In high-firing, you sever your draining connection with the person, but you do it from a high intention. The intention is that both you and the person prosper through severing the connection.

There is a convenient rule of thumb for determining who needs to be high-fired. Fire anyone who costs you time, energy, or money three or more times.

Take a moment to think of who in your world fits that category.

Listen to a Corporate Mystic describe the process of high-firing: "One day at a meeting my partner and I had a revelation. We realized that we had spent considerable time that week patching up a communication breakdown caused by one of our salespeople lying and failing to keep agreements. We applied the high-firing rule of thumb to the situation: Had things like this happened at least two times before? The answer was a resounding 'yes.' So we decided to high-fire him. To get clear on our intentions, we had to look at why we had kept him around so long. The answer was illuminating. My partner and I had both grown up with alcoholic fathers, so we were used to covering up the messes made by others, out of our love for them. We were treating our salesman like our fathers! That came as a real shocker to realize this, because the salesman was actually younger than we were.

"We wrote out an intention on a piece of paper. It said 'We release our connection to Bob in a way that allows us all to prosper.' Then we called Bob in and told him everything we had decided, including even the part about our alcoholic fathers. To our surprise, Bob burst into tears and confessed that he had been stealing trivial things from the company in a way we had never suspected. He also told us he hated putting on a suit and tie each day because he liked to spend time outside. The upshot was that he ended up thanking us as he left. Later we heard that he had set up a small lawn-care outfit. The bottom line to us was that it seemed like our whole company breathed a sigh of relief."

Everything in the universe is subject to change
and everything is right on schedule.

—A Corporate Mystic

PART THREE

THE DISCIPLINED MYSTIC: FOUR TEN-MINUTE PRACTICES FOR ENHANCING INTEGRITY, VISION, AND INTUITION

Learning the information in this book is useful, but mastery becomes possible only when you practice it in key situations. It is easy to have integrity, vision, and intuition when things are going well, but only practice will keep them in place when the pressure is on.

The following practices are designed to be done in ten minutes or less. If you have more time, they can be amplified with great value.

THE BASIC CENTERING PRACTICE

Many of the Corporate Mystics we interviewed are staunch advocates of meditation in some form. Not all of them call it that, but they are really talking about the same thing: a method of clearing and quieting the mind so that it becomes refreshed, creative, and productive. We were surprised to find that quite a few top corporate executives have been trained in one of the formal approaches to meditation such as Transcendental Meditation, Zazen, or Vipassana; others have invented a practice for themselves that works.

In our seminars and consultations with corporations we began to teach meditation twenty years ago when it was much less accepted than it is now. We did so with trepidation, because we feared that it would be met with resistance. Indeed there was resistance on occasion, but much less so than we imagined. Once people practiced meditation, they immediately recognized how beneficial it could be. The Basic Centering Practice, which follows, has stood the test of time, becoming our favorite generic meditation technique, one which uniformly yields excellent results.

This practice will teach you how to bring about a clear feeling of balance and ease in your body very quickly. In studying what makes people feel off-center, we found three commonalities in their experience. First, when people feel off-center, their stomach muscles are usually tense. This is not surprising. All animals tighten their stomach muscles when they're afraid, so this habit probably started for many of us in childhood as a response to fear. Certainly today's business climate has many things about it that trigger fear. Fear is nothing to be ashamed of, and can actually be a useful ally. Fritz Perls, the psychiatrist who founded Gestalt therapy, said that fear was merely "excitement without the breath." Take a few breaths, he counseled, and you will feel your fear turn into excitement.

Second, breathing tends to be shallow and high in the chest. This breathing pattern is part of the fight-or-flight reflex, wired into our bodies over thousands of years of dealing with stressful situations.

Third, people feeling off-center usually tell us that their minds are scattered and overly busy.

We developed the Basic Centering Practice as a way to correct each of these problems directly. You will find that even a short practice of it will quiet your mind and make your body more relaxed.

Use it by itself whenever you want a sense of calm well-being. It also can be used as a prelude to each of the other three activities in this section.

INSTRUCTIONS

Get comfortably seated. Arrange it so you won't be interrupted for the next ten minutes. You can do the practice with eyes open or closed; experiment with each way to find out which brings about the deepest sense of ease.

STEP ONE

As you breathe slowly out your nose, tighten your stomach muscles, particularly the ones right around your navel. Keep them tight until all the breath is out of your body, then relax your stomach muscles completely as you breathe in. Take a slow deep breath as deep down into your abdomen as you can get it. As you breathe slowly out, tighten the muscles around your navel again. When all the breath is out of your body, relax your stomach muscles completely as you breathe in. Repeat this procedure several more times, tightening your stomach muscles on the out breath and relaxing them on the in breath. After several cycles, rest and take your mind off your breathing for a few moments.

STEP TWO

Now, return your attention to your breathing. Breathe slowly and deeply, keeping your stomach muscles very relaxed. Count silently in your mind as you breathe in and out: in-two-three-four, out-two-three-four, making each number equal to about a second. Each in breath will take about four seconds and each out breath will take the same amount of time. Do several cycles with this four-count. When you feel that you can take a longer breath, go to a five-count: in-two-three-four-five, out-two-three-four-five. Do several cycles with the five-count. Always stay in the comfort zone: Keep the breath easy and peaceful.

Eventually, if you are able to do so comfortably, extend the count to six, seven, or eight. Always stay in the comfort zone. The lighter and easier you can make the breath, the more centered you will feel.

STEP THREE

When you feel centered, let go of the counting and the focus on your breath. Just relax for a minute or two, letting your mind and body enjoy the quiet sense of balance and well-being.

Meditation is just focus.
We all know how to focus
on exterior things in our lives.
Meditation is a focus on the inside.
It's trained my mind not to run away on me.
I believe that 90 percent of what most people think
is fantasy created by our runaway minds,
and it's not real.
When the mind is focused,
you can concentrate on what is really meaningful.

—ED MCCRACKEN

YOUR INTEGRITY WORKSHEET: THE F·A·C·T PROCESS

The purpose of the Integrity Worksheet is to crystallize all the essential integrity teachings into one concentrated and highly usable form. You can apply the Integrity Worksheet to any problem, large or small. It was originally designed to break up corporate logjams, and it has done so successfully many hundreds of times. It is our hope, though, that you will apply it before the logjam stage is reached. If you use it preventively rather than waiting until a crisis develops, you can smooth out situations in ten minutes that might take months to handle otherwise. The steps in the process are:

- Facing
- Accepting
- Choosing
- Taking Action

Most people find it useful to write down their responses, but it can also be done in the mind's eye.

INSTRUCTIONS

STEP ONE: FACING
The first step is to face the situation as it stands now. Twenty-five hundred years ago the Buddha said, "All human unhappiness comes from not facing reality squarely, exactly as it is." It is a wise, even crucial observation for us today.

The Questions: What is the reality of the situation? How would I like it to be? Are there ways I or others are out of integrity?

♦ The reality of the situation—the way it is now—is

_____

_____

- My goal—how I'd like things to be—is

    _____
    _____

- Have I communicated anything untrue in the whole course of this situation?

    To myself:

    _____

    To anybody else:

    _____

- Have I broken any agreements in the course of this situation?

    With myself:

    _____

    With others:

    _____

- If untruths or broken agreements have come to light, the action step(s) I will take to rectify them is:

    _____

    By when?

    _____

STEP TWO: ACCEPTING

Once you have faced the issue squarely, you are ready for the step of acceptance. Complete acceptance of a situation, exactly as it is, creates an openness to change.

The Question: What about this situation have I not accepted, exactly as it is?

_____
_____

- Is it something about myself?
- Is it something about someone else?
- Is it something in the past?
- Is it something that's happening now?

Take a moment now to accept it, just as it is.

STEP THREE: CHOOSING

Once you have faced and accepted a situation thoroughly, you are in a clear position from which to choose how you would like things to be.

The Question: What do you most want in this situation?

_____

_____

STEP FOUR: TAKING ACTION

Once you have faced, accepted, and chosen, the next step is to design the actions that are required.

The Question: What action(s) can you take to support your getting what you most want in this situation?

_____

_____

I commit to taking the action(s) by _____

FUTURE-VISION

This activity has emerged from our workshops as one of the most powerful ways of getting everyone to become a visionary. The purpose of future-vision is to get comfortable in an imagined future. It is not important that your visions of the future be accurate or feasible. The goal is simply to become conversant with the future, to have the flexibility of mind to "unstick" yourself from the bounds of time. Future-vision teaches this skill by encouraging you to locate yourself in an imagined future and operate as if that future had already happened.

This activity is best done in a team. Three is an ideal number, so that you can have a future-visioner, a facilitator, and a scribe. In our workshops we switch roles so that everyone has a chance to be future-visioner. The job of the facilitator is to read the instructions to the future-visioner and to ask the questions. The scribe's job is to take notes that can be shared later in a discussion. The scribe has an important task, because most people forget half of what they said if they really get into the activity.

The activity can also be done alone, although it may be harder to surrender yourself to it. The following instructions are based on doing it in a team of three.

INSTRUCTIONS

Pick who will be future-visioner, facilitator, and scribe. The facilitator gives the instructions.

STEP ONE
The facilitator says: Choose a goal, issue, or problem that is significant for you. A goal might be something like the successful launch of a new product, while a problem might be something like what to do about an employee who isn't performing well. Pick one and jot it down on a piece of paper.

STEP TWO
The facilitator says: Select a place in the room that you can let represent the future. Get comfortable there, seated or standing. Throughout the activity do

your best to stay in the imagined future. Close your eyes and really imagine that you are in the future, when the goal has been achieved or the problem successfully solved. Get the feeling in your body that it was a total, unqualified success.

I'm going to ask you some questions. Do your best to answer them from the future, as if the goal has been achieved or the problem solved. The scribe will keep track of your answers.

- What is it that makes this a total success?
- What is the positive effect that this success is having on people?
- What did you learn about yourself of most value that allowed you to contribute to the success?
- What did other people learn of most value that allowed them to contribute to the success?
- What were the course corrections that might have thrown you and others off-course before that this time you navigated successfully?
- If you had to pick one thing, what did you and/or your team do that created this successful outcome?
- If you were to give one piece of advice to us back here in (name today's date), what would it be?

STEP THREE

Take a moment to relax, then come back to the present and let's talk about what you experienced.

(The scribe reads back the notes from the future-visioner's answers. After discussing these, change roles and do another round.)

THE INTUITION PRACTICE

This practice is the most reliable way the authors have found for turning on the power of intuition. It is a seeding technique in which you plant a question in your mind, then let go and receive what comes. Sometimes you will get imagery, sometimes words or concepts. Oftentimes you will get nothing at all right away. Be patient, though, because something useful may appear that night in a dream or the next morning while you are in the shower.

INSTRUCTIONS

STEP ONE
Select a goal, problem, or issue to focus on. Phrase it in the form of a question, as in "How could I best handle the GE account?" Jot your question down on a piece of paper. Get comfortable (use the Basic Centering Practice) and arrange it so you will be undisturbed for the next ten minutes or so. This process tends to work better when your eyes are closed, but feel free to experiment to find which works best for you.

STEP TWO
When your mind is quiet, float your question in your mind and then let it go. Let go of any expectation and get receptive. Take any images that come up or any ideas that emerge. Receive them nonjudgmentally; you can sort them out later.

Enjoy your mind and how it works. You might enjoy looking for the open space between and behind thoughts. If you do this for a moment, the open space will actually seem to grow larger. Relax into this space. Accept it.

STEP THREE
When you get to a good stopping place, open your eyes and jot down what you have received. Open the interpretive part of your mind and apply it to what images and ideas have emerged. Look for patterns, metaphors. If nothing you consider useful has emerged, let go for right now and open yourself to something coming along later.

THE LAST WORD

"Any last words of wisdom you can give us?" the student asked.

The mystic thought for a moment. "You can work out just about any difficulty you have by remembering two sentences."

"What are they?"

"Number one: What is, is. Number two: What isn't, isn't."

The mystic continued: "A lot of people waste their time focusing on what isn't—they dwell on things that aren't real. If something's real, if it actually is—whether it's a feeling like anger or a fact like sales are down—it's a waste of time wishing it wasn't. What you do if something is real is accept it just like it is, then decide if you want to put the energy into trying to make it different. Once you decide you want to try to change it, then put your energy into what needs to be done. That's everything you really need to be successful in business and life."

No matter what your past has been,
you have a spotless future.

—Tony Hsieh,
CEO, Zappos

Everyone is in the best seat.

—John Cage

THE SEVEN RADICAL RULES FOR BUSINESS SUCCESS

Here they are the stripped-down essential rules for business success, derived from over one thousand hours of illuminating interviews and conversation with highly successful corporate leaders. They are radical for two reasons: They will produce a revolutionary change in your life and working relationships, and because they go to the root (that is the original meaning of *radical*) of what is wrong in most businesses.

Rule One

Always tell the truth. Especially tell the truth about personal facts and feelings. Make everything possible in your business open book. Teach everyone how to read the spreadsheet, make all salaries public, never hide anything that is not absolutely required to be hidden.

Rule Two

Always take 100 percent responsibility for any activity you're involved in. If you are in a leadership position, take 100 percent, not 200 percent for all activities. Require that each participant take 100 percent. Equality is possible only through meeting at the 100 percent level.

Rule Three

Scrupulously attend to all agreements you make and others make with you. Do everything you say you are going to do, and don't do anything you've said you wouldn't do. Demand impeccability of others. If you catch yourself or others in a broken agreement, cop to it immediately and fix it.

Rule Four

Never gossip and never get in the middle of communications between other people. Make your no-gossip commitment public, and state your intention to stay out of the middle of conflicts and communication glitches.

Rule Five

Set aside daily creative think-time and make it sacred. It doesn't matter if it's five minutes or an hour. What matters is that your intention is to renew your connection with your inner spirit and open to your full creativity. Find your own preferred method: Meditate, deep breathe, sit quietly, doodle. If you miss a day, do twice as much the next day.

Rule Six

Make a to-do list and update it constantly throughout the day. Put your most dreaded activities first and do them first thing.

Rule Seven

Go to the source. Whenever you hear of something that makes you feel uncomfortable, talk to all parties concerned and listen carefully to them. Let people have the ten minutes of clear communication that solves most problems. Listen with as little agenda as you can manage.

FOR FURTHER INFORMATION

GAY HENDRICKS is the author of more than forty books about the power of human transformation, including such classics as Conscious Loving and The Big Leap. After receiving his Ph.D. from Stanford in 1974, he became a professor of counseling psychology at the University of Colorado, retiring in 1995 to direct The Hendricks Institute. Dr. Hendricks and his wife, Dr. Kathlyn Hendricks, have worked together for forty years and have appeared on more than 500 television and radio programs. Information on their programs can be found at www.hendricks.com

KATE LUDEMAN and her husband and business partner Eddie Erlandson offer executive coaching, team building, and keynote speeches through her firm, Worth Ethic Corporation. Information on these and other individually tailored services is available by emailing her at Kate@WorthEthic.com.

ABOUT THE AUTHORS

GAY HENDRICKS is the author of more than forty books about transformation. After receiving his Ph.D. from Stanford in 1974, he became a professor at the University of Colorado, retiring after twenty years to direct his own consulting firm, The Hendricks Institute, whose fifteen associates have worked with several hundred organizations worldwide.

KATE LUDEMAN is an engineer with a doctorate in psychology. An executive coach, she is the author (with her husband Eddie Erlandson) of *Radical Change, Radical Results* and *The Alpha Male Syndrome*. Among the many clients of her firm, the Worth Ethic Corporation, are Dell, Sysco, eBay, Microsoft, General Electric, Johnson & Johnson, and the Gap.

Printed in Great Britain
by Amazon